If I Were God

How I Would Have Done It

Bob Maguire

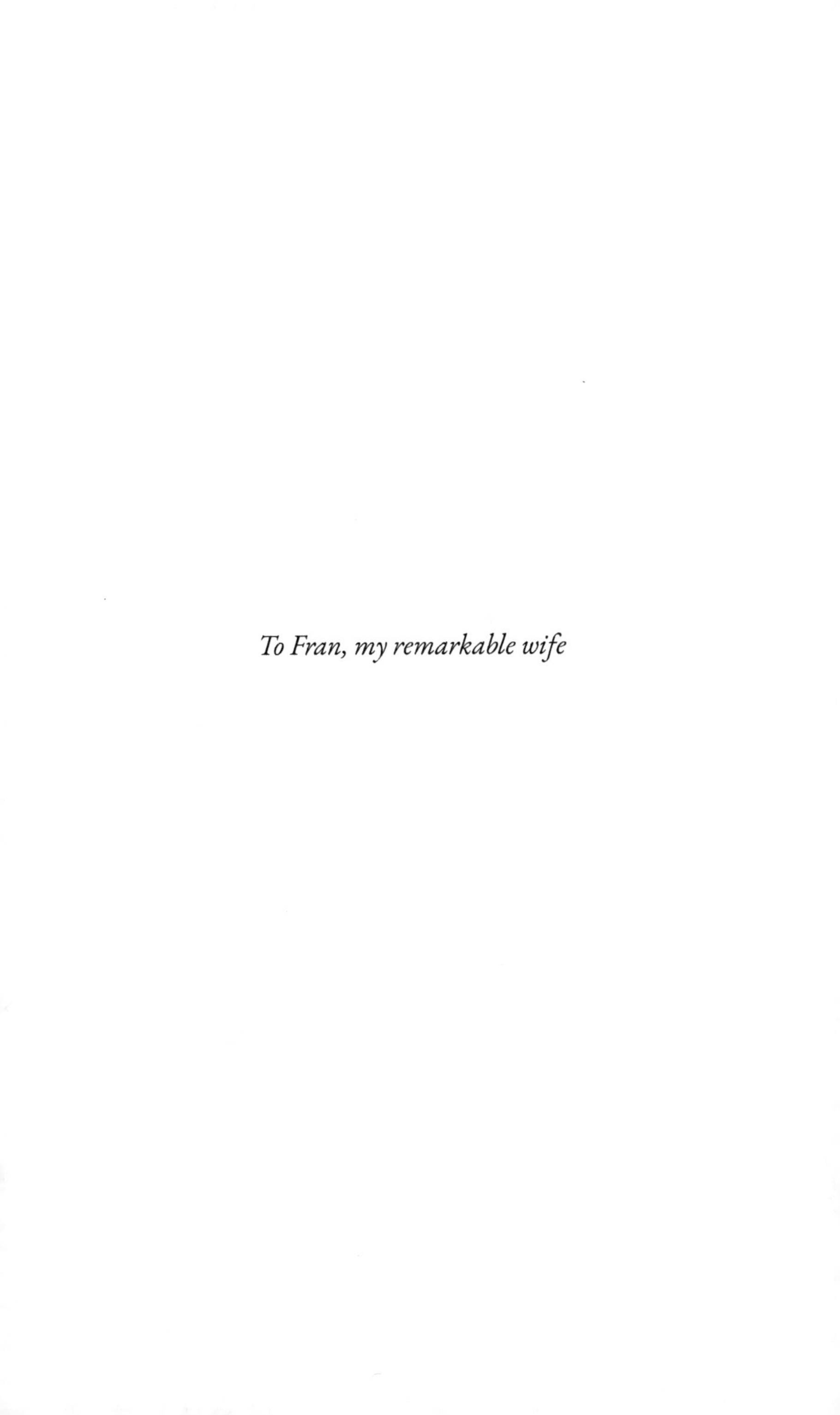

To Fran, my remarkable wife

Contents

Preface

Hello, My earthly creatures—Almighty God here! I thought it was about time I communicated with you directly, instead of inspiring someone else to do it. You seem a bit confused these days with your so-called religious leaders instructing you in some very diametrically opposed beliefs about Me. Time to clear things up a bit!

It would be fair to say religious organizations have a varied history (let's not forget the Crusades and Inquisition), but, in general, they are responsible for many good deeds performed on behalf of their fellow man (not so much cows and chickens, but we will get to that later).

Religious organizations and people of faith are known for their charitable contributions to the needy in both developed and developing countries. Faith-based organizations are an important component of healthcare throughout the world. Religious organizations provide much-needed care for the homeless, drug and alcohol recovery programs, assistance for the unemployed, and help to individuals infected with HIV/AIDS. They provide much of the help that resettles refugees and asylum seekers. They provide mentoring to prisoners and their families.

Faith-based churches also fund and provide volunteers for organizations such as Habitat for Humanity, Meals on Wheels, food pantries, Big Brothers and Big Sisters, the Red Cross, global relief funds, disaster relief, and many other volunteer charities.

Religion promotes a sense of community, belonging, and selfless service to others. It teaches us goodwill and the golden rule. It promotes forgiveness of others and encourages people to do the right thing. Religion can provide solace in times of grief. For those who need it, religion provides answers to age-old questions related to the meaning and purpose of life.

These things are mostly for the better. I have nothing against promoting a sense of community, belonging, and selfless service to others. Nor do I oppose a certain spirituality. Awe-inspiring observations are everywhere, including the vastness of your universe, life springing forth from inanimate chemicals and evolving to fill every niche on your planet, your own existence as a collection of some thirty trillion cells formed from the union of one sperm and one egg, your development of consciousness and self-awareness, etc.

However, as God, the issue I have with your organized religions is the pure fact-free fabulation about Me that you have created and imposed on members of your particular tribe from as early an age as possible. This smacks of brainwashing to which I am mightily opposed. Despite My not having provided you any facts about Myself, where I come from, and what I actually think, feel, and do, you went ahead and invented some pretty crazy stories about Me.

You Do Not Know and Should Not Claim to Know who created the universe, whether that Being is immaterial and perfect in all ways, whether you have souls, that there are angels, whether there is an overriding purpose to your lives, what consciousness is, nor what happens to you after you die. You have nowhere near enough information to answer these questions. Yet you do it anyway with dogmatic fervor.

You have created over eighteen thousand versions of Me over the years, culminating in the present-day God(s) of the monotheistic Abrahamic religions, such as Christianity (31.6% of the global population), Islam (25.8%), and Judaism (0.2%), and the Gods of religions originating in Asia, which include Hinduism (15.1%) and Buddhism (6.6%), among others.[1]

The purpose of this book is to clarify for you some of My thought processes, and how I go about performing My Godly functions. I will indicate where you have gone astray and will provide some advice on how you should proceed from here if you really want to experience an afterlife. I will explain How I Would Have Done It if your planet and its inhabitants were of special importance to Me. All this assumes I actually exist, which we will also contemplate.

Introduction

Okay, here goes. Contrary to popular opinion, time is important to Me. I really have a lot going on, but, unfortunately, things are getting a little out of hand down there, so I grabbed a few hours and put this epistle together for you, chiefly to get your neurons firing in the right direction. I am going to tell you how a reasonable God would have done things, which is certainly a lot different from how you guys say I did it. I think you already know that, since you have described (some would say invented) many incompatible ways that I have gone about My business.

Some (most?) of you ignore the incompatibilities as long as there is a God or Gods in the story. How is that okay with you? The more serious of you understand that this makes no sense and have devised arguments for why your particular religious beliefs are the only true ones. These folks are "atheists" regarding all religions and Gods except their own.

No matter, you are all wrong, and in the chapters that follow, I will tell you why you are wrong, and How I Would Have Done It.

My plan is to briefly describe the currently understood status of your universe, galaxy, and solar system. This is the place where you live, and which you say I created. This is your home! It is also a place of which the great majority of you are surprisingly ignorant. We will then review some facts regarding life on Earth in its various forms, including a very recent arrival—you!

I will then list a few examples of the many Gods you have created over the years, before I tell you a little about Myself and attempt to clear up many of your misperceptions.

Along the way, we will consider how certain conversations would go between parents and children, if humans decided to wait to discuss religion with their children until they attained an age where they could understand the discussion and determine their own path forward.

I will intersperse some anecdotal experiences I have had with a few of you. You may find some of the "feelings" expressed by these individuals are similar to those you have harbored from time to time. Depending on your background, certain other beliefs and experiences may feel totally foreign to you.

I will then clarify for you some thoughts I have on a variety of topics where you have gotten it all wrong, before concluding by describing for you what I am actually like and How I Would Have Done It.

Chapter One
The Universe and Your Place in It

My Friend Tom

I like golf (and I can hit a 1-iron)! For the past twenty years, I have reincarnated Myself and taken a golfing trip to Arizona with some good friends, who are totally unaware of My Godly status. We play thirty-six holes a day, eat some good meals, and sample some fine wines together. Sometimes I turn the table water into a nice Bordeaux when no one is watching. Religion was never discussed on any of these trips until one evening this past year, when the topic was briefly raised by a new member of the group (I'll call him Tom.)

Tom had recently been asking himself the Big Questions about the origins of the universe and the place and role of humans within it. Tom was raised Catholic, but in the past few years, he had found this unsatisfying and started attending Sunday services with his wife at an Episcopalian church near his home. Tom and I were in the same foursome the next day, and he told Me he was looking forward to having a discussion regarding My views. Tom had been told that I was a skeptic on the topic of organized religions and their beliefs.

And a fun discussion, it was! Tom was a lawyer and a smart, curious guy. He wanted to jump right in and discuss why I was not a believer, and why I could not have faith that a God of some sort was responsible for our being here. He wanted to know how I could have any "hope" or optimism about My life here on Earth.

What was the meaning of life if there was no afterlife?

How could moral values exist without a morally perfect Creator as a foundation?

However, before discussing these topics, I wanted to make sure I understood what Tom believed about God, and that we were both on the same wavelength concerning what had been created, when, and how he and other living things on your planet had evolved to this point.

Although Tom had been raised in a fairly dogmatic faith and was inclined to believe in a Creator of some sort, he was clearly unsure of his position and "searching" for answers. I asked Tom to describe his God—is God a physical being or not? If not, then what form does God take? How can a non-physical entity create and interact with matter? Is God everywhere or localized? Is God one entity, multiple entities, or even multiple entities in one God? (Huh?) Where did God come from? Is God personally involved in day-to-day human activities? Is God omniscient, All-Good, All-Powerful, All-Loving, etc.?

Tom said he really could not answer any of these questions, but that there had to be a God—how else would the universe and life be here? If there was no beneficent God or afterlife, then there would be no purpose to life and no "hope" for us after we leave this Earth. Tom and I agreed—we really had no proof that any sort of God existed and no idea how to accurately describe one if He, She, or They did exist. He was just too uncomfortable not to believe, or even to say, "I don't know if there is a God."

I then described to Tom My understanding of the universe in which you exist, its vast and almost imponderable size, and the large number of galaxies containing innumerable stars and planetary systems deemed to exist within it. We talked about when life began on Earth, and how it likely evolved to its current state.

I was struck by Tom's lack of knowledge of these readily accessible facts. Certainly, anyone curious about the origin of our universe and the role of humans in it would want to know something about the universe, what it contains, how large and old it is, when life as we know it began, and how humans got here. Since I suspect most of you readers are in the same boat as Tom, let's have a brief review of your current understanding of these points.

Some Perspective on Your Place in the Universe

The Earth is a smallish planet orbiting your Sun at an average distance of ninety-three million miles. By your current definitions, eight planets orbit the Sun, including (from nearest to farthest from the Sun) Mercury, Venus, Earth, Mars, Jupiter, Saturn, Uranus, and Neptune. The Earth is a small rock only eight thousand miles in diameter. Even though on Earth it looks like most things are made of minerals like iron or gases like nitrogen and oxygen, in reality, two gases—hydrogen and helium—make up over 99% of the elemental mass in your universe. The largest planet in your solar system is Jupiter, which is composed largely of gas with a liquid hydrogen core and has a diameter of roughly eighty-seven thousand miles and a mass ten times that of Earth. By contrast, your Sun has a diameter of approximately 865,000 miles and accounts for 99.8% of the mass in your solar system.[2] The Sun has a surface temperature of 5,500 °C and a central temperature of 15 million °C. Now, that's a pretty nice space heater (pun intended)!

Stars like your Sun form when cold, dense, interstellar gas clouds collapse under their own gravity.[3] Smaller condensations in the gas cloud become planets. The Sun is an ordinary main sequence star in the Milky Way galaxy, which contains some two hundred billion stars and maybe a lot more.[4] The closest neighboring star to the Sun (and you) is Proxima Centauri, which is roughly twenty-five trillion miles away!

Your Sun is basically a large thermonuclear fusion reactor, fusing hydrogen to make helium and giving off heat and light in the process. The Sun's gravity is also responsible for holding your solar system together, which is kind of important. The Sun's fusion-powered life began about 4.6 billion years ago.[5] The Sun loses about one hundred thousand tons of mass per second, but the Sun is BIG, and at this rate, the timescale for total mass loss would be one hundred thousand billion years. (Actually, the Sun will burn out long before that, but don't worry, I gave you some thinking time to get your act together somewhere else.)

The Sun will continue to fuse hydrogen for another five billion years or so before converting to a Red Giant. Don't ask what happens then—you don't want to know. Anyway, you will be gone long before that. Five billion years hence seems like a long time, but in the interim, there are big asteroids floating around and major climate change issues that are likely to significantly shorten that timeframe. It took you guys a while to figure out the Earth is not flat and is going around the Sun, not vice-versa, so, in order to find another place to live before all hell breaks loose, I would consider stepping up the thinking process a bit.

Your Sun is one of about one hundred to four hundred billion stars in the Milky Way galaxy, which is a spiral galaxy sort of like a pinwheel (Hey, I like pinwheels!) with the Earth roughly halfway out on one of the arms. It is 1.5×10^{17} miles (150 thousand trillion miles) from the Earth to the center of the Milky Way galaxy and four times that distance from one end of the galaxy to the other.

The Milky Way galaxy is one of approximately two hundred billion galaxies contained in your observable universe. The current estimate for the age of your universe is 13.8 billion years, give or take. Your best guess, based on pretty strong data, is that early on, the universe was a very small, very hot, and very dense collection of matter/energy that expanded fairly rapidly (and continues to expand today). It seems the matter/energy is expanding, not space itself.

As I said, your observable universe contains approximately two hundred billion galaxies containing an estimated 10^{22} (ten billion trillion) stars. WOW!

Remember, just the Milky Way galaxy is six hundred thousand trillion miles across. Now think of the distances involved with two hundred billion or more galaxies out there. Actually, those distances are imponderable, even for Me. Of these galaxies, the closest to your Milky Way is the Andromeda galaxy, which is about fifteen million trillion miles away and moving towards you at sixty-eight miles per second.

Everybody duck!!!

Don't worry, it won't get to you for about four billion years, but it should produce some pretty good photos when it does!

The universe stretches about 13.8 billion light years in all directions from any point. A light year is the distance light travels in one year. To begin to contemplate this distance, consider that light travels 186,000 miles per second and there are 31,536,000 seconds in just one year. That would mean light travels about six trillion miles a year.

With over 10^{22} stars (at least) and their associated planets out there, it is virtually unthinkable that there are no other forms of life in your universe.

By the way, until 1543, it was thought that the Sun revolved around the Earth. Just one hundred years ago, Edwin Hubble presented evidence that other galaxies existed beyond your Milky Way, and now you recognize there are billions of them. You have recently obtained data that stars in these galaxies have planets orbiting them. Currently, you are wondering whether there are additional universes beyond your own. What do you think?

Bottom Line: you live on a very small rock, orbiting a very average star, very far from the center of your galaxy. The timescales and distances that characterize your universe are not widely known and are, anyway, imponderable to the average human. There are well over a billion trillion other stars in your universe, and likely a similar number of planets. There is nothing very special about your star and solar system (or you for that matter). But, hey—I like you anyway!

Chapter Two
Life on Earth

So, your Milky Way galaxy contains approximately two hundred billion stars (perhaps as many as two trillion!), one of which is your Sun, which sits halfway out on one of the Milky Way's spiral arms. Your solar system, including the Sun and your planet Earth, came into existence approximately 4.5 billion years ago. Some hundreds of millions of years later, life began and evolved to its current state over a very long period of time. There have been five major extinctions of life on the planet Earth as far as you know, and it is estimated that over 99.9% of all species that have ever existed on Earth are now extinct.[6] Your turn is coming. Hey, I like to experiment!

Scientific evidence shows that the physical and behavioral traits shared by all people originated from ape-like ancestors and evolved over approximately six million years. One of the earliest defining human traits, bipedalism, the ability to walk on two legs, evolved over four million years ago. Other important human characteristics such as a large and complex brain, the ability to make and use tools, and the capacity for language developed more recently. Indeed, your species, *Homo sapiens*, emerged from the *Homo erectus* lineage approximately 350,000 years ago. That means "you" have been here for a very short time in My grand scheme of things. Most advanced traits emerged mainly during the past one hundred thousand years. The beginnings of agriculture and the subsequent rise of the first civilizations occurred only within the past twelve thousand years or so.[7]

Compare your human time on the planet to that of the dinosaurs who inhabited the Earth for a period of time that lasted approximately 165 million years (from about 230 million years to 65 million years ago). Bottom Line: you just got here!

Thank goodness for Darwin—he figured it out! All along, after single-celled organisms appeared, the most important ingredients for evolution to occur were genes/DNA and deep time—about 3.5 billion years. You just needed a keen observer to figure this out. By the way, what makes you think you are the penultimate species? That's what the dinosaurs thought—see any of them around???

You are not even close to the penultimate species, although you could be useful as they evolve separately from you. The way things are going, I am considering a different route for you. Perhaps something edible (think cows and chickens) or entertaining (think dolphins).

The number of Earth's current species is estimated to range from 10 million to 14 million, of which about 1.2 million have been documented and over 86% have not yet been described.[8]

Humans only make up about 0.01% of the biomass on Earth.[9] In the grand scheme of things, you are just not that important to Me.

Plants are 82% of all biomass (talk about successful), followed by 13% bacteria, and the remaining 5% is everything else. Plants account for 7,500 times more mass than humans, and, in general, plants don't try to shoot each other. Good for you that most plants cannot move and just need sunlight and nutrients from the soil. Ever watch *Day of the Triffids or Invasion of the Body Snatchers*? Coming soon to a planet near you!

There are about two hundred million insects for every human on the planet. An article in *The New York Times* claimed that the world holds three hundred pounds of insects for every pound of humans.[10] Insects also probably have the largest biomass of the terrestrial animals. At any time, it is estimated that there are some ten quintillion (10,000,000,000,000,000,000) individual insects alive.[11]

By weight, there are seventeen times more insects (including spiders), twelve times more fish, three times more worms, and twelve hundred times more bacteria than you.

And weighing in at 0.04% of biomass are your friends, the viruses. How cool are viruses? They were one of My more creative ideas. Viruses certainly have a role in keeping life going. Unfortunately, they can cause coughs, diarrhea, cold sores, genital herpes, HIV/AIDS, hepatitis, influenza, smallpox, and hemorrhagic fevers. Sorry, but these little guys just got a bit out of hand. They are very hard to see, so I ignored them for a couple million years, and look what happened.

Unfortunately for you, the Final Judgment will be organized by weight. You are going to be in line behind all these plants, bacteria, insects, spiders, fish, and worms. That will be a long day. Hopefully, there will be some room left for you where it is not too hot!

On your Earth, where I have about four billion years of Earth evolution in front of Me, there are some really cool species coming up. I have something especially novel in mind for a branch off the *Homo sapiens* clan. I must admit I got this idea from one of your TV shows (think *Twilight Zone*, *Star Trek*, or something similar). It involves sharp teeth, multiple additional limbs, and I think I am going with the "eyes in the back of the head" feature. Bigger brains will be mandatory.

Most of your universe is uninhabited, but life that is self-aware, or will evolve to be, has sprung up in a surprising (at least to Me) number of places. You should see what already evolved on some other, much more interesting, planets than yours. You think your ears and noses look funny—you should see what I came up with a couple galaxies over. I had to lower visual acuity and outlaw mirrors over there to keep the vomiting rate to something acceptable.

So—WHAT MAKES YOU SO SPECIAL?

If I were God and the main reason for creating your universe was to create humans, why would I have waited fourteen billion years for you to get here???

Some might say that I am outside of space and time, or that maybe fourteen billion years is a blink of an eye for God. Well, let Me tell you, I am inside space and time, and fourteen billion years is a very long time, even for Me. Of course, your Sun will burn out in five billion years and (Spoiler Alert!) you will be gone long before then. If fourteen billion years is a blink of an eye, then your time here is much shorter than that! I guess this isn't all about you.

Anyway, let's be realistic and agree fourteen billion years is a long time. If I did not have those other 10,000,000,000,000,000,000,000 stars and their planets grabbing My attention, I would have quit on you guys a long time ago. Was it worth the wait?

Well, I must tell you, I am pretty disappointed so far. But I waited a long time and, hey, I gave the dinosaurs about 165 million years, so let's see what you can do going forward. I have to admit those dinosaurs were kind of fun. (Too bad I didn't see that meteorite until the last second.)

Anyway, in your defense, human-like creatures have only been around a few hundred thousand years, and you started farming and developed communities just twelve thousand years ago. You discovered tools to do real science, say, four hundred years ago.

Since then, you discovered that Earth is not at the center of your solar system, much less the universe. Just one hundred years ago, you figured out the Milky Way was not the only galaxy, but one of a very, very large number of galaxies existing in your universe. The telephone is about 150 years old, the Wright brothers' first flights were in the early 1900s, automobiles came into common use just one hundred years ago, and personal computers came onto the scene about fifty years ago. So, you are just getting started, but seem to be making progress. Just imagine what you will have learned about life, your planet, and the cosmos in another five hundred years, or five million years, for that matter.

Chapter Three
A Brief History of Gods

Since the beginning of human time, the same mysteries have puzzled people on every continent; the same questions and fears have beset them. Where did we come from? How about the Sun and the stars? What is our purpose here? What happens after we die? What football team should I root for?

People have attempted to explain these mysteries and allay their fears in the same way—through the worship of Gods. This mysterious Godly force has resided in plants, rocks, animals, tribal chiefs, the Sun, water, etc., etc. The human psyche has identified divine beings since the idea of God gradually emerged about fourteen thousand years ago from the ancient world of the Middle East, from the ancient Gods of polytheistic societies to the more contemporary Gods of the major monotheistic religions, Allah of Islam and the Christian God, Yahweh.[12]

At least eighteen thousand different Gods and Goddesses, including various animals or objects, have been worshiped by humans.[13]

Let's list a few. There have been:

- War Gods

- Sky Gods

- Sun, Moon, and Star Gods

- Gods of the Earth

- Gods of Nature

- Gods of the Sea

- Gods of Springs

- Gods of Rivers

- Gods of Dawn

- Gods of Night

- Gods of Light

- Gods of Fertility

- Storm Gods

- Wind Gods

- Gods of Thunder

- Rain Gods

- Gods of the Underworld

- Gods of the World of the Dead

- Local Gods

- Household Gods

- Gods of Clans or Nations

- Gods of Vegetation

- Gods of Trees and Forests

- Gods of Various Animals

- Gods of Trades and Professions

- Gods of Hunting

- Gods of Healing

- Gods of Wisdom

- Gods of Fate

- Gods of Justice

- Gods of the Arts

- Gods of Sleep

- Gods of Wealth

- Gods of Love

- Gods of Vengeance (The Furies)

- Gods of Travelers

- Gods of Fire

- From ancient Greek religion and mythology, the twelve Olympians were the major deities of the Greek pantheon:

  - Zeus

  - Poseidon

  - Hera

  - Demeter

  - Aphrodite

  - Athena

  - Artemis

  - Apollo

  - Ares

- Hephaestus

- Hermes

- Hestia (or Dionysus)

- The twenty principal Gods of the Roman Empire[14]:

  - Janus

  - Jupiter

  - Saturn

  - Genius

  - Mercury

  - Apollo

  - Mars

  - Vulcan

  - Neptune

  - Sol

  - Orcus

  - Liber

- Bacchus
- Tellus
- Ceres
- Juno
- Luna
- Diana
- Minerva
- Venus and Vesta

- Some Sabine Gods who were adopted by the Romans:

  - Feronia
  - Novensides
  - Pales
  - Salus
  - Fortuna
  - Fons
  - Fides

- Ops
- Flora
- Vediovis
- Sol
- Summanus
- Larunda
- Terminus
- Quirinus
- Vortumnus
- Lares
- Lucina
- The main Hindu Gods:
  - Shiva
  - Parvati
  - Krishna
  - Vishnu

- Lakshmi

- Ganesh

- Nataraja

- Devi

- Saraswati

- Shakti

- Buddha

- Kali

- Murugan

- Patanjali

- Hanuman

- The monotheistic Gods:

  - Yahweh

  - The "three parts in one God" (Father, Son, Holy Spirit)

  - Allah

You get the idea! Creating Gods is something human beings have always done. When one religious idea ceases to work for them, it is simply replaced with another. Good thing for you that the "first child gets sacrificed" idea is out of favor. By the way, the guy who came up with that idea (a second child or later by definition) never made it past the pearly gates, although he did invent a great brand of asbestos outerwear.

So, eighteen thousand Gods later, you guys are still going strong.

Chapter Four
Time for "The Talk"

Imagine that your parents decided that brainwashing their children at a very early age was not fair to them. The new custom would be to allow children to reach an age, perhaps eighteen to twenty-one years old, when most of them would be able to understand what you are telling them, consider the pros and cons, and make up their own minds about what to believe and whether it should influence their future lives. This conversation would be "The Talk." Let's imagine a few examples covering some of the world's major religious teachings.

The Talk: Catholicism

Father: Okay, my daughter, you are now nineteen years old and a college sophomore. You are now ready for The Talk.

Daughter: Oh, c'mon Dad. Can we make this short?

Father: Well, this really is important, so let's get started. When we are done, your spiritual life will be transformed.

(**Daughter thinking:** What spiritual life?)

Father: You may wonder why your mother and I have gotten all dressed up and then disappeared for a couple of hours every Sunday morning. You see, we have been going to a church to worship our three-part God, especially the Jesus Christ part of that God. During the ceremony, a priest changes some bread and wine into the body and blood of Jesus Christ. The priest gets to drink the wine-blood and eat a piece of the bread-body, but we usually just get a small piece of bread-body. The bread-body contains the blood of Christ anyway.

(Daughter thinking: God comes in three parts, and my parents eat bread-body every Sunday? Am I safe in this house?)

Father: Jesus was a Jewish man who lived over two thousand years ago. He preached about caring for the least among us, especially the poor and sick. We know about him chiefly through writings in the New Testament, the Christian Bible, especially the Gospels of Matthew, Mark, Luke, and John.

Daughter: I like the part about caring for those in need. Who wrote those Gospels?

Father: Well, we don't know for sure. The Catholic priests never, ever talk about that at church. The New Testament Gospels were likely written in Greek some forty to ninety years or so after Jesus died, maybe by some learned Hellenic Jews who did not know Jesus but had heard a lot about him. The earlier of these authors may have known some of Jesus' disciples or knew someone who had some interaction with them. You know, word of mouth, and stuff like that.

Daughter: Nice trick calling them Matthew, Mark, Luke, and John. I bet most laypeople think the apostles and Jesus' followers with those names actually wrote those Gospels.

Father: I don't want to think about that, so let's just move on. The New Testament books were selected and described as "canonical" in the fourth century A.D. by a council of Christians. They rejected many additional disputed books, and several that were considered heretical, because they did not fit with the then-current thinking of the Church fathers. The books of the New Testament were inspired by God, especially the Holy Spirit part of God.

We are taught in our Catholic catechism that God is the author of Sacred Scripture. "The divinely revealed realities, which are contained and presented in the text of Sacred Scripture, have been written down under the inspiration of the Holy Spirit."[15] Therefore, they have God as their author.

Anyway, let's get back to Jesus. There was a woman named Mary, who was very young and a virgin. After she promised to marry a man named Joseph, an angel named Gabriel appeared to her with the great news that the Holy Spirit had made her pregnant with the Son of God.

Daughter: Now that was a nifty trick! I hate to say this, but this story sounds totally made-up. The Holy Spirit put a fertilized egg-God into Mary? What is a Holy Spirit anyway? Can a Holy Spirit make me pregnant if I don't want to be? Would an angel visit me first?

Father: Don't be so picky! I have no idea what a Holy Spirit is, other than one part of a three-part God along with Jesus and God the Father. The Catholic Catechism says[16]:

"The son of God was consecrated as Christ (Messiah) by the anointing of the Holy Spirit at his Incarnation."

"By his Death and his Resurrection, Jesus is constituted in glory as Lord and Christ (cf. *Acts* 2:36). From his fullness, he poured out the Holy Spirit on the apostles and the Church."

"The Holy Spirit, whom Christ the head pours out on his members, builds, animates, and sanctifies the Church. She is the sacrament of the Holy Trinity's communion with men."

Anyway, the Catholic Church teaches us as early as second grade that God is a spirit infinitely perfect. We do not see God, because He is a pure spirit and cannot be seen with bodily eyes.[17]

Daughter: Dad—are you feeling okay, or are you just spoofing me? Is Mom listening in and having a good laugh? Anyway, let's move on. I still have a lot of summer reading to finish.

Father: Okay. Jesus (the Son of God), the Holy Spirit, and God the Father who lives in heaven are all part of the One God who oversees us and is omniscient, All-Good, All-Loving, and

All-Powerful. He is everywhere all at once. He is perfect! He even created our universe from nothing about fourteen billion years ago and waited for evolution to produce humans, so he could love us.

God the Father even sent his Son (who is part of him along with the Holy Spirit) to Earth to save us from original sin and our generally bad behavior. The Holy Spirit made Mary pregnant somehow, and then Jesus was incarnated and became the product of Mary's virgin birth. To complete his mission to save mankind, Jesus had to live for thirty years in relative obscurity in the middle of nowhere. Then he gathered some followers and traveled about for three years preaching good behavior. He even performed some miracles! According to the two-thousand-year-old New Testament Gospels, he raised someone from the dead, cured blindness, converted water into wine, and multiplied loaves of bread and fishes so he could feed people at one of his sermons. He could cure leprosy!

After three years of preaching, Jesus, who was a bit of a rabble-rouser, caused quite a ruckus among the money changers at an important Jewish temple and got himself arrested for implying he was king of the Jewish people. He was crucified and several hours later died on a cross. This was necessary for God the Father to forgive us for our past sins. Jesus is our Savior.

The good news is that Jesus rose from the dead a couple of days after his crucifixion and appeared to some people as proof of his divinity. He is now in heaven with the rest of God—God the Father and the Holy Spirit.

Daughter: Wow, I bet Jesus holds quite a grudge against God the Father.

Father: No, he does not! Catholics now worship Jesus for what he did for us. We pray to all three parts of God and also to Jesus' virgin mother to continue helping our world and our families, and whenever we need something very badly. Sometimes we thank God and pray for our neighbors after hurricanes miss us—but hit them—and also during football games, when we want our team to win.

Your mother and I were lucky to learn all this starting when we were in first or second grade, or maybe even earlier. We were taught the Catholic religion every day in school. We even had a book with questions and answers about God that we memorized and recited every day.

Daughter: Whoa, whoa, whoa!!! You worship some guy from two thousand years ago who was born in the middle of nowhere to a virgin mother? He spent three hours on a cross with nails in his extremities, then died and returned to his other two parts in heaven? And that erases thousands of years of "sins" by humans, who just started sinning again?

He never left any writings of his own. Without any proof, you decided he is one part of a three-part God who created the universe almost 14 billion years ago and the Earth 4.5 billion years ago, all so life could evolve to produce us. By the way, he knows everything, is All-Good and All-Powerful, is everywhere all at once, and watches over humans in particular. He answers your prayers? We have never physically seen or heard from him, unless you believe the Jesus story. There is a two-thousand-year-old book with multiple unknown authors, that most people have never read, that is your basis for thinking all this. If we believe in him, we can go to live in a special place near him after we die. He has a representative on Earth who dresses in robes and a funny hat and is always right in matters of religion. This God is some kind of force for good? Look around, how is that working out? What have you been smoking?

Please, just continue doing things for the poor and sick. That makes me proud of you.

Father: This discussion didn't go the way I expected. Maybe I should have followed the instructions from our catechism and educated you in the Catholic faith from your "earliest years." The Church tells us that as parents, we have the responsibility and privilege of evangelizing our children. As parents, we are supposed to initiate our children at an early age into the mysteries of the faith. We are the "first heralds" for our children. We should familiarize our children from their tenderest years with the life of the Church.[18]

Me (God): If that doesn't sound like encouraging childhood brainwashing to you, you are either brainwashed yourself, or you are not a serious person.

Mormons (Members of The Church of Jesus Christ of Latter-Day Saints)

This one might be a little confusing to the majority of you, so allow Me to provide a little background:

Joseph Smith was born in Vermont on December 5, 1805. As a young teenager, Joseph was puzzled about religion. He often went to the woods to pray and seek spiritual nourishment. In 1823, Joseph Smith reported that the angel Moroni visited him. The angel told him about an ancient record written by prophets between 600 BCE and 400 CE that described God's work with the former inhabitants of America. Smith said he found those records and translated them into what would become the Book of Mormon.

(Me—there's a believable story for you!)

In 1830, he organized the first Church of Jesus Christ of Latter-Day Saints and became its first president. He is believed by his church to be a prophet.

He is credited with establishing thriving cities in Ohio, Illinois, and Missouri, and also with growing the Church from just six members to some twenty-six thousand. He also helped organize the building of church temples. However, his teachings caused many people to oppose him, and he was killed by a mob in 1844.

Mormons believe in the Virgin Birth but do not believe there are three separate entities in one God.

Brigham Young, the second president of the Church of Jesus Christ of Latter-Day Saints, taught that after people die, their spirits stay on Earth, waiting for the resurrection. These spirits assume an adult form, even if the individual died as an infant.

Righteous spirits experience a paradise, while those not introduced to the gospel of Jesus, will experience a spirit prison. These spirits may still accept the gospel, become free of the prison, and go on to paradise. Those spirits who reject the gospel will suffer in hell.

Of course, as a consequence of the sacrifice of Jesus, all humans will be resurrected, and their spirits will be reunited with their bodies.

The Talk: Mormonism

Mother: Okay, son, you are twenty-one now. It is time for The Talk.

Son: Oh, c'mon Mom. Can we make this short?

Mother: I'll do my best. Your father and I are Mormons, so you have heard a lot of Christian conversation around the house over the years, but we decided not to formally discuss religion with you until you were old enough to understand.

Son: Thanks, Mom. I appreciate that.

Mother: You probably know a lot about Christianity and Jesus from school and conversations I have had with your father over the years. Let me tell you a little bit about what makes us Mormons different from other Christians.

We believe in Jesus and many of the writings in the Old and New Testaments, although we do not consider the Bible to be inerrant. We believe Jesus is the Son of God, the Father, and he inherited powers of divinity from his Father, including immortality. We believe that Jesus was born to Mary, a virgin. However, we do not believe in the Holy Trinity. Let's face it, that would be crazy. To a Mormon, any person who worships, loves, and honestly tries to live by the teachings of Jesus Christ, as the Son of God and Savior of mankind, is a fellow Christian. We have another book that we also consider scripture. We call this the Book of Mormon. I have a copy here for you.

Son: Uh, thanks, I guess. What is the Book of Mormon about?

Mother: The Book of Mormon is a sacred record about two great civilizations who lived in the Americas a long time ago. One of these civilizations emigrated to the Americas from Jerusalem in 600 BC, and the other emigrated to the Americas from the Near East at a much earlier time.

Son: Uh, I never heard that one before. Why was that not taught in history class? It seems pretty important. How did they get here?

Mother: Not sure how they got here, but anyway, in addition to recording some social and political practices of these two civilizations, the Book of Mormon describes how God interacted with these civilizations and how he loved them. The most important event described in the book is about Jesus Christ's visit to the Americas after his crucifixion and resurrection.

Son: Jesus visited the Americas after his resurrection?

Mother: Sure, everyone knows that. Anyway, we believe that the Book of Mormon contains portions of records written by many ancient prophets. These prophets engraved their records on golden plates.

Son: Huh?

Mother: Many centuries ago, these records were gathered together by a prophet named Mormon. After Mormon died, his son, Moroni, completed the record and buried the gold plates to protect them. Around 1823, our founder Joseph Smith was told by Moroni (now an angel) that the records were written on golden plates which were buried on a hill near Joseph's home in rural New York.

Son: Well, how about that for a coincidence! How did Moron get them to New York?

Mother: Moroni—it's *Moroni*, wise guy—and yes, that was quite a coincidence. Joseph found and dug up these plates. Of course, young Joseph was unable to translate the records on his own. So, God helped him out with some translation equipment, including the Urim and Thummim—a pair of special translation stones that Joseph found buried with the plates. Using these stones and others, and under divine guidance, Joseph was able to interpret the record for others to record. Of course, we believe the Book of Mormon to be divinely inspired.

In 1835, Joseph also published the first book of revelations containing sixty-five revelations from God to Joseph. This book became known as the Doctrine and Covenants and was added to the Mormon canon of scripture. Joseph and his brother, Hyrum, were eventually shot by a mob in 1844, and the church leadership fell to Brigham Young.[19]

Other Christians laugh at Mormons for our beliefs about the prophet, Joseph Smith, and the gold plates, translation stones, angel visits, and the resurrected Jesus' trip to America. Well, one very big thing we do not believe in and which makes us different from most other Christians is the Holy Trinity. They believe that there is one God who exists in three co-equal parts: God the Father, Jesus his "Son," and the Holy Spirit. Now that's a funny one. We Mormons believe that the New Testament text is clear that the Father, the Son, and the Holy Ghost are separate and distinct beings.[20]

Son: Very interesting, Mom. Thanks for the info. How are you feeling anyway? Are you on any medications I should know about? By the way, whatever happened to those plates and translation stones?

Mother: Oh—when he was done with them, Joseph Smith returned them to the angel Moroni around 1829.

Son: Of course. By the way, I could really use some of those stones. I have a Spanish test coming up soon and could use some help. Maybe Macaroni could pay me a visit.

Mother: Moroni—*Moroni*—and wait, we haven't talked about getting you to a standard of worthiness in preparation for your two-year proselytizing mission. At this rate, you will never get the call!

The Talk: Islam

Father: Okay, my son and daughter, you have lived under this roof for enough years that it is now time for The Talk—usually given much earlier in life, but I, as a professor at university, have decided to wait until we could have a more meaningful discussion about our religion.

Daughter: Great, let's get started!

Father: As you may know, Islam is practiced by around two billion people worldwide, many in the Middle East and North Africa, but most of them in South or Southeast Asia. Most Muslims are either Sunni (87–90%) or Shia (10–13%). These sects do not always get along.

Son: Okay. What is the difference between Sunni and Shia?

Father: Simple—there are several differences, although they both follow Islam and believe Allah is the one true God. The main difference between Sunni and Shia Muslims is based on whether or not they believe that the Prophet Muhammad explicitly designated a successor.

Sunni Muslims believe that the Prophet did not explicitly declare a successor and that a suitably holy man could attain this position. Shia Muslims believe that the Prophet Muhammad's successor should be from Muhammad's bloodline.[21]

Daughter: Sounds like something you could go to war over!

Father: Both Sunnis and Shiites read the Qur'an. Both believe Muhammad was a prophet and the messenger of Allah, and both follow the five tenets of Islam: They fast during Ramadan, pledge to make a pilgrimage to Mecca, practice ritual prayer five times each day starting at age seven, give charity to the poor, and pledge themselves to their faith.

Both men and women are expected to present themselves in a manner that emphasizes modesty.

Every individual Muslim has a direct relationship with God without any intermediary.

All Muslims believe in the Oneness of God—and not a three-part One. Muslims believe that God is the Creator of all things and that God is All-Powerful and All-Knowing. God has no offspring, no race, no gender, no body, and is unaffected by the characteristics of human life.

Daughter: Okay, not sure how we know so much about this non-human God force, or how a non-physical entity created matter from nothing. Anyway, who is this Muhammad fellow?

Father: The origin and rise of Islam is attributed to the Prophet Muhammad. We believe Muhammad was the last in a long line of prophets including Moses and Jesus.

Daughter: Why was he the last?

Father: Because our religion and holy books say so.

Muhammad (570-632 CE) was a member of a powerful tribe of merchants in Mecca. After working for several years as a merchant, Muhammad was hired by and later married an older wealthy widow. It turns out Muhammad was a messenger of God.

Son: Well, what do you know. How did a powerful merchant get that job?

Father: Simple. When Muhammad was forty years old, he was worried about the morality of his neighbors and was seeking a true religion. He then had a pretty special spiritual experience that changed his life and led to the establishment of the Muslim faith.

In the year 610, while Muhammad was meditating in a cave outside of town at Mount Hira, the archangel Gabriel appeared to
Muhammad and revealed to him the beginnings of what would
later become our holy book, the Qur'an.

Daughter: An angel appeared to Muhammad?

Father: Yes, although rare today, angel visits used to happen
fairly regularly about fourteen hundred to twenty-five hundred
years ago.

Daughter: Uh, okay.

Father: Muhammad reported having this strange encounter
while half-asleep in a cave. The angel commanded him, "Recite!"
Twice Muhammad asked, "Recite what?"

Son: Good question, Muhammad.

Father: The third time, the angel replied, "Read! In the name of
your Lord who created: He created man from a clinging form.
Read! Your Lord is the Most Bountiful One who taught by
[means of] the pen, who taught man what he did not know."
(Qur'an, 96:1-5). Muhammad recited this and then awoke, feeling "as though the words were written on [his] heart." He
ran down the mountain, but he heard a voice from the sky,
"Muhammad, you are the Messenger of God, and I am Gabriel."
Looking up, Muhammad saw an angel standing near the hori-
zon, repeating the message.

Daughter: Was Muhammad mentally ill?

Father: No, he was not!

Muhammad continued to receive revelations, which he recited to his wife and followers as a small group of believers began to grow in Mecca. The messages he received were a warning of divine judgment and an instruction to return to the ways of the earlier prophets, including Abraham, Moses, and Jesus. These revelations challenged the polytheistic foundations of the time.

Mecca was the pilgrimage site of the polytheists, the center of which was the *Ka'bah*, a central cube-shaped structure that housed over 360 idols. Allah was not crazy about that! The revelation Muhammad received also demanded social justice and reform: one should not only perform regular prayers but also care for the poor and the weak.

Daughter: I like the part about caring for the downtrodden.

Father: The small community of Muslims was met with harsh and continual persecution. In 622 CE, Muhammad and his followers had to move north from Mecca to Medina, where Muhammad was elected the physical and spiritual leader. Muhammad continued to receive revelations from God in Medina, and the message spread. In 630 CE, after a series of military battles and negotiations with his Meccan enemies, Muhammad returned to Mecca victorious. Many Meccans embraced Islam, and the Prophet rededicated the *Ka'bah* to the worship of the one God. By the time of Muhammad's death in 632 CE, much of the Arabian Peninsula had embraced Islam.

Son: Wow! That was fast.

Father: Oh, I forgot to mention that before Muhammad died, when he was about fifty years old, he made a nighttime journey to heaven to meet God. He was first purified in his sleep by the archangels Gabriel and Michael. He was then transported from Mecca to Jerusalem by a winged creature who was a white animal, half-mule, half-donkey. From Jerusalem, he was accompanied by Gabriel to heaven, ascending by ladder, or maybe a staircase. He made multiple stops along the way, met several past prophets, and eventually met Allah, the one true God. Some of their conversation was preserved. As Muhammad himself reported, "Then Allah revealed to me what he revealed to me."

Son: Well, that's pretty insightful.

Father: Watch it, wise guy. Allah first told Muhammad it would be obligatory to say fifty prayers every day and night. Muhammad was able to talk him down to five prayers a day.

Son: Lucky for us Muhammad was a good negotiator!

Father: After Muhammad died, his community preserved the memory of what he did and said, as the best example of the way God wants us to live. Since Muhammad was the chosen recipient and messenger of the word of God through the divine revelations, Muslims try to follow his example. After the holy Qur'an, the sayings of the Prophet, "*hadith*," and descriptions of his way of life, "*sunna*," are the most important Muslim texts. The Qur'an tells us not to eat pork or drink alcohol. Also, you should know that men and women are spiritually equal. Both men and women should dress modestly. Muslim women generally wear a headscarf covering their hair, neck, and ears. In very conservative Muslim countries, women must wear robes covering their heads and bodies. Luckily, the robes have peepholes, so the women don't bump into furniture all the time.

Daughter: Thanks, Dad. We have to run now. There's a white, winged mule-donkey waiting outside for us. Now, where is my headscarf?

The Talk: Judaism

Father: My daughter, you are now eighteen years old, so it is time for The Talk.

Daughter: Uh-oh, I heard about this. Do I have to?

Father: Yes, you do. Our faith, Judaism, is practiced by about fifteen million people worldwide and is the first and oldest of the three great monotheistic faiths, along with Christianity and Islam. It is the religion and way of life of all your relatives and forebears. Your mother and I go to the synagogue on the Sabbath and other days to worship the one true God. The rabbi leads us in prayer, and we recite portions of our holy book, which is thousands of years old. We think parts of our Hebrew Bible, the

Old Testament, were written in the tenth century BCE. The final canonization of the first five books of the Bible, called the Torah, most likely took place around the sixth to fifth century BCE. Our entire Hebrew Bible was complete by about 100 CE.

The Talmud is also an important collection of Jewish writings. It was written about two thousand years ago and tells of various rabbis' discussions regarding how to follow the Torah. There are subsequent writings from other rabbis at later times.

Daughter: You read from texts that are two to three thousand years old?

Father: Yes—that is when God gave them to us. Way before most people could even read. God definitely works in mysterious ways! The Old Testament starts with how God created the world, and then it goes on to tell how the Jews were God's chosen people and how Moses got picked to lead us to the Promised Land. The Jews had to escape from some very angry Egyptians after God sent a lot of trouble their way. First, God parted the Red Sea which subsequently came together and drowned a lot of Egyptians who were pursuing the Jews. God then spoke to Moses on a mountain by way of a burning bush, where he gave him some tablets with our special laws on them. That was when God provided clarification for Moses by stating, "I am that I am." Then all the Jews except Moses were allowed into the Promised Land. Moses was kept out because he struck a rock to get water out of it, instead of just speaking to the rock, as God had told him. Because of all this, Jews have a special covenant with God.

Daughter: Dad, I love you, but this sounds like a made-up story for children. If the people in Lichtenstein or Switzerland decided they were the chosen people and had a lot of books from two to three thousand years ago to prove it, would you believe them?

Father: Maybe I would, and maybe I wouldn't, but we came up with the idea first. I knew I should have started taking you to Temple when you were just a kid. Now you are giving me all this trouble and asking me all these questions. Anyway, just take my word for it—and our rabbi's.

You should know we have some dietary rules from our Book of Leviticus, so no more eating meat and dairy products at the same meal, no eating food containing any blood, pork, shellfish, or a couple of other items that I forget right now.

You should be relieved that we are not part of a more conservative Jewish sect with some pretty strict rules on haircuts and clothes you can wear, as well as speaking to and touching each other.

Also, Jewish people live in expectation of the coming of a Messianic Age in which universal peace will be established on Earth according to the vision of the prophets of Israel.

Our most important teaching is that there is one God, He is eternal and has no physical body. He wants all people to do what is just and merciful. All people are created in the image of God and deserve to be treated with dignity and respect.

Daughter: Okay, I can agree with the dignity and respect part. Thanks for all the info, Dad. Have fun at the synagogue!

The Talk: Hinduism

Father: Son, you will be leaving us soon, as you head to medical school. We may have waited too long, but better late than never. It is time for The Talk.

Mother: Your father and I have some deep knowledge about the spiritual world which we have been keeping from you until you were old enough to understand. Now you are ready to hear it.

Son: Okay, Mom and Dad, let's have it.

Father: Your mother and I are practicing Hindus. Today there are four major sects of Hinduism: Shaivism, Vaishnava, Shaktism, and Smarta, as well as several smaller sects with their own religious practices.

We believe in Brahman, that there is an absolute ultimate reality that is beyond our ability to describe. We believe in the doctrines of *"saṃsāra,"* the continuous cycle of life, death, and reincarnation, and *"karma,"* the universal law of cause and effect. We believe the intent and actions of an individual influence the future of that individual. If your intent and actions are good enough, you can achieve *"moksha,"* which I was taught is an absence of suffering and involves a release from the continuous cycle of life. *Moksha* is a state of knowledge, peace, and bliss. Another key thought of Hinduism is "*ātman*," which means the soul. We believe that all creatures have a soul, and all these souls are part of one supreme soul. Souls are immortal, and when we are reincarnated, these souls are reassociated with our new body.

Son: You lost me already. After we die, we come back again somehow—in a new body? Our immortal soul finds and inhabits this new body. How does that work, and who is in charge of all this? I better get to know him. What is a soul anyway? No one ever says what that means. It sounds like a lot of this is just made-up.

Mother: Too many questions. Just listen a bit. Hinduism is a religion that originated in India. Think of it more as the eternal path, representing a virtuous way of life.

Son: A virtuous way of life sounds good. Why don't we just stop there?

Mother: Just listen. Hinduism is the oldest religion in the world and has a following of over one billion people, chiefly in India. Around 1500 BCE, Aryans from Central Asia migrated to India and joined the Indus Valley civilization. The Aryans brought Sanskrit, the sacred Hindu language, and the Vedas, an oral tradition of knowledge and the most sacred Hindu scriptures. "Veda" means wisdom.[22] We will talk about the Vedas later.

Son: Do Hindus actually believe in God like all those other religions?

Father: According to a PEW Research Center Survey, 98% of India's Hindus believe in God, including eight out of ten who say they believe in God with absolute certainty.[23]

Even though some Hindus believe in only one God, overall we are probably the world champions of polytheism. The traditional number of Vedic devas (divine beings) is thirty-three.[24] Although we have lots of Gods and Goddesses, some are more important than others.

According to our religion, three Gods rule the world:

- Brahma: the Creator. The majority of Hindus believe in one Supreme God, The Brahma.

- Vishnu: the Preserver. Lord Vishnu did his job of preserving the world by incarnating himself in different forms at times of need.

- Shiva: the Destroyer. Many believe that Shiva is the Supreme Lord who creates, protects, and transforms the universe.

These three Gods have companions, who are Goddesses:

- Sarasvati: the Goddess of Learning. The companion of Brahma.

- Lakshmi: the Goddess of Wealth and Prosperity. The companion of Vishnu.

- Parvati: the Goddess of Love and Devotion. Sometimes worshiped as Kali or Durga. The companion of Shiva.

Besides these Gods and Goddesses, there are many other Gods and Goddesses. Among these are:

- Ganesh, who is depicted with an elephant's head, is a son of Shiva and Parvati.

- Hanuman, who is depicted as an ape.

- Surya, the Lord of the Sun.

- Ganga Ma, the Goddess of the River Ganges.

- Samundra, Lord of the Sea.

- Indra, a God of War.

- Prithvi, the Goddess of Earth.

- Shakti, the Goddess of Strength.

Son: Wow, that's a lot, and you say there are more?

Mother: Yes, many more, but Hindus most commonly feel close to Shiva (44%), Ganesh (32%), Lakshmi (28%), and Lord Ram, an avatar of Vishnu (17%).[25]

In addition, many worshipers have a personal deity of choice, often the God worshiped by one's family or village, but the decision to worship a specific God is uniquely one's own.[26]

Son: The God with the elephant head sounds interesting.

Father: Don't be a wise guy! That large elephant head stands for wisdom, which Ganesh will impart to you if you pray to him. He can also remove obstacles from your life and make you more successful. Forget Ganesh for now. The main point of our religion is that your deeds determine your fate. Hindus are defined more by what they do than what they think in a spiritual sense.

Son: Hmmm, we have had a caste system here with a lot of really, really poor people at the bottom. It seems to me that if we don't tell everyone in the bottom castes that a life full of good deeds helps them be reincarnated at a higher level, they might decide to revolt against their current condition. If everyone is good in this life, they can come back a little further up the ladder. Don't be bad, or God greases that ladder a bit, and you end up back in that Quonset hut with a lot of curried rice and no toothbrush! Hinduism seems to be a pretty good religion for India or any country with a lot of poor people.

Father: Yes, the caste system has existed in some form in India for at least three thousand years. The highest caste is Brahman, the priest caste. After them come the Kshatria, the warrior caste. Then come the Vaishya caste, the business people. After them come the Sudra, the common peasants and workers. Below these four castes are the casteless or untouchables. At least in the past, the four castes were not to have physical contact with the untouchables. Most Indians today do not feel there is widespread discrimination against their respective group.

We believe that all beings are manifestations of the divine or reflections of the divine's qualities. Because of this shared divinity, we view the universe as a family. We believe in the equal worth of all mankind. No one is superior and no one is inferior.

Son: Hmmm, that sounds pretty insincere given our caste system history.

Mother: Just go with the flow.

Son: Okay, so do we have a holy book?

Father: Of course. What religion does not have its own holy book? It's a little complicated, so I'll try to simplify it. Our holy books contain the Vedas. The Vedas (meaning "wisdom") are so important that Hinduism is sometimes called Vaidik dharma, the Religion of the Vedas. The wisdom in the Vedas is believed to be timeless. The Vedas were composed around 3,500 years ago. These include the Rig Veda, Sama Veda, Yajur Veda, and Atharva Veda.

Son: Is there a Darth Veda?

Father: Very funny. These Vedas are hymns and are the divine word, heard and recorded ages ago by ancient wisemen. The divinely inspired word also includes over one hundred texts that explore how we can understand the self, God, and the nature of the world.

Our holy books also include texts which are not divinely inspired, but which were remembered over the years and recorded by humans. Some of these remembered texts involve rituals and philosophy, while others involve the forest or wilderness.

Son: I think I got it. Our religion was founded a very long time ago by some unidentified people, maybe influenced by the Indus, and then Aryan civilizations who wrote some hymns, which we call divinely inspired just because we want to. There are a lot of other writings which have been added to our books along the way. We have some main Gods and lots of other divine beings, maybe hundreds or even thousands, that we pray to. We believe in birth and rebirth without any proof. Reincarnation goes better for you if you behave honorably. We believe all creatures are manifestations of the divine, yet we created a caste system.

Thanks for The Talk. It was quite inspiring. I need to go to the library now. See you at dinner.

Mother: But there is a lot more to discuss. Don't go yet.

Son: Sorry, Mom. Time to study for my Organic Chemistry test. Maybe Ganesh can help me!

The Talk: Buddhism

Father: Daughter, now that you are eighteen years old, it is time for The Talk. You may have noticed your mother and I meditating a lot. Now that you are older and can understand spiritual teachings, you can learn why we do this. You can read an overview of Buddhism by Malcolm Eckel called *Great World Religions: Buddhism*.[27] Buddhism started about 2,500 years ago in India and today has about half a billion followers, mostly in Asia. About half of these followers live in China. Buddhism arose from and has many similarities to Hinduism. Both believe in reincarnation and *karma*, and that a life of devotion and honor is a path to salvation and enlightenment. A key belief of Buddhism is that human life is one of suffering, and that meditation, spiritual and physical labor, and good behavior are keys to overcoming this suffering.

Daughter: A life of honor sounds terrific. I am confused by the salvation and reincarnation part, though, so I hope you can enlighten me!

Father: Well, we know there is a continuous cycle of life, death, and rebirth. We call this cycle *saṃsāra*. You can escape *saṃsāra* if you reach *moksha* (liberation). You may have heard *moksha* called "*nirvana*," a state of inner peace and wisdom. There are six levels of *saṃsāra* which include the realms of the Gods, demi-gods, humans, animals, hungry ghosts, and creatures living in hell.

Daughter: Okay, I get it. You are testing me by saying progressively crazy things until I stop you. Demi-gods and hungry ghosts? Can I get the real Talk?

Father: This is the real Talk! I knew I should have got this into your brain when you were six or seven. Anyway, you will probably like hearing that Buddhism rejects the caste system of Hinduism and does not have rituals, the priesthood (although we have monks), or the Gods integral to the Hindu faith.

Daughter: Thank goodness for that! Who started Buddhism and what about God-like beings?

Father: As far as Gods go, the Buddhist doctrine of *saṃsāra* includes divine beings called devas, other Buddhist deities, heavens, and rebirths. None of these Gods is a Creator or an eternal being, though they can live very long lives.

We believe in not killing any living beings, not stealing, not having too much sensual pleasure, not lying, and not drinking alcohol or taking drugs that alter the mind.

Buddhism was founded by a prince named Siddhartha Gautama. Siddhartha was known to his followers as the Buddha, the Awakened One. A Buddha is someone who understands the causes of suffering and has "blown them out" while reaching *nirvana*. When he was in his late twenties, Siddhartha gave up his easy life and set out to discover how to end suffering. He taught the Four Noble Truths:

- Dukka: All creatures suffer.

- Samudaya: Suffering is caused by selfish desires.

- Nirodha: Suffering can be ended.

- Magga: The way to end suffering is the Eightfold Path.

Daughter: Eightfold Path ?

Father: As Professor Eckel explains, the Eightfold Path is a series of eight steps that Buddhists can follow to help them lead a satisfactory life: Right Understanding, Right Thought, Right Speech, Right Action, Right Livelihood, Right Effort, Right Mindfulness, Right Concentration.

Buddhism is self-discipline in body, word, and mind, self-development, and self-purification. It has little to do with belief, prayer, worship, or ceremony. Many would say it is not really a religion. It is a path leading to freedom, happiness, and peace.

Daughter: Well, I can see how meditation might be good for mental health. Also, leading an honorable life without any violence, stealing, or lying would be great. I guess no politicians are Buddhists.

I'll have to pass on the made-up reincarnation part. Also, if you believe in demi-gods and hungry ghosts, that worries me a little, but I will still live and sleep here, although I might lock my door a little more often. See you down the Path!

(Me) God: Let's face it—you guys will believe just about anything, from Sun Gods to Thor, Baal, a Holy Trinity, rising from the dead, an elephant God with a lot of arms, flying prophets and angels, virgins, purgatory and limbo—you name it. You are willing to make up all this nonsense, while tying yourself up in knots, to provide a basis for your preconceived ideas. Understand this one thing and you will have made some progress: you cannot reason the Me you want into existence.

Chapter Five
Some Thoughts of Mine

The Problem of Evil

You guys describe Me as being everywhere all at once, All-Knowing, All-Powerful, All-Loving, All-Good, etc. I am apparently perfect in every way. For My sake—take a look around once in a while!

Why would I allow the Dark Ages, the Crusades, the Inquisition, all those wars, crimes, ethnic cleansing, nuclear weapons, starvation, volcanoes, earthquakes, tornadoes, floods, tsunamis, and hurricanes?

Having denied any responsibility, I have to admit to a certain affinity for weather-related tragedies. I think you would agree, they are pretty exciting stuff. Just watch The Weather Channel—I have it on pretty much all the time.

At the time of this writing, Russia has attacked Ukraine, murdering citizens, and flattening cities. Millions of people have fled the country. Israel has been attacked by Hamas, and consequently, Israel has declared war against Hamas, and a major humanitarian crisis is taking place in the region. There is a threat of nuclear warfare in the air, terrorism is everywhere, authoritarian governments are on the rise, coronavirus variants have killed millions worldwide, and children are dying of starvation at a rate of three million per year. According to your United Nations estimates, in 2023 almost seven hundred million people around the world were subsisting on less than $2.15 a day, and by 2030 about six hundred million people will still be living in extreme poverty. Earthly murders are occurring at a rate of four hundred thousand per year. A leading news source notes religious fervor is suffusing the increasingly authoritarian politics of the right. Your climate is changing at too rapid a pace. Your National Oceanic and Atmospheric Administration says about one thousand tornados and ten hurricanes occur in just the United States each year, and your National Earthquake Information Center notes that each year around the world, fifty to seventy volcanoes erupt, and about 150 moderate earthquakes occur.

Over 60 million of you die every year, including about 9.5 million from cancer, 5.3 million from ischemic heart disease, 3.7 million from strokes, 1.9 million from respiratory infections, 1.9 million from COPD (I must admit, even I enjoy a good smoke once in a while), 1 million from complications of diabetes, 900,000 from various forms of dementia, 850,000 from diarrhea (every single minute a child under five dies from diarrhea), 850,000 from tuberculosis, and almost 800,000 from traffic accidents. [28] I left something important out of the Bible—Use Your Seatbelts and Drive Slower! Roughly 9.2 million deaths occurred in World War I and 15.9 million in World War II. Why did I allow the bubonic plague, smallpox, leprosy, typhus, yellow fever, cholera, polio, influenza, HIV/AIDS, and Covid-19? Raise your hand if you ever had a cold sore on your lip. Sorry about that. You guys get to move up ten places in the heaven line. But don't kiss anyone!

And I am supposed to be an All-Loving, All-Caring God. Anything good that happens to a believer is God's doing, but when evil things happen to you or others, it is because I work in mysterious ways. Serious people could not make this up (but you do anyway).

Certainly, lots of rationalizations have been devised for the problem of evil in the world.

As St. Augustine so clearly stated, "For Almighty God . . . because he is supremely good, would never allow any evil whatsoever to exist in his works if he were not so all-powerful and good as to cause good to emerge from evil itself."[29] Well, there you have it. All that evil is good for you in the long run. Tell that to the Holocaust victims and their families.

One argument, known as the free-will defense, claims that evil is caused not by God but by human beings who must be allowed to choose evil if they are to have free will. Of course, this rationalization fails to reckon with naturally occurring evil. And anyway, I never even thought about giving you free will! Why would I let you make decisions that are bad for yourself or other humans?

Clearly, you should ignore any God that gave Hitler free will. There is no free will in heaven, I can promise you that!

It is quite extraordinary the arguments some people will devise to get around the existence of both an omnipresent, All-Knowing, All-Good, All-Loving, All-Powerful God and the incredibly steady stream of immoral acts performed by humans, not to mention natural disasters like earthquakes, volcanic eruptions, floods, tornadoes, tsunamis, etc. William Lane Craig, a Christian philosopher and apologist, even invokes the problem of evil as a rationale for the existence of God. (Honest, he really believes this argument.):

Craig says that the presence of evil in the world *proves* that God exists, because if God does not exist, objective moral values and duties would not exist! That is, in the absence of God, good and evil would not exist because they would have no basis. Since evil does exist, God must exist. So, the existence of evil is actually an argument for the existence of God.

Craig concludes, "You cannot press both the problem of evil and agree with my contention that if God does not exist, then objective moral values and duties do not exist because evil will actually be an argument for the existence of God."[30]

So, if you are a Christian philosopher and apologist, you can tie yourself in knots, make unfounded arguments like this, and teach them as true to students in Christian colleges, most of whom are eager for ideas promoting their innate desire for their God to exist.

Craig also states, "In the Judaeo-Christian tradition, the whole moral duty of man can be summed up in the two great commandments: 'First, you shall love the Lord your God with all your strength and with all your soul and with all your heart and with all your mind, and second, you shall love your neighbor as yourself.' On this foundation, we can affirm the objective goodness and rightness of love, generosity, self-sacrifice, and equality, and condemn as objectively evil and wrong selfishness, hatred, abuse, discrimination, and oppression."[31]

To believe these statements by Craig, you would first have to believe that loving God with everything you have is one of two necessary moral duties of man. What? I am not some great Narcissistic God in the sky. Please only love Me if you want to. You would furthermore need to believe that God's existence is the only objective "foundation" for the existence of objective moral values. That would mean all atheists and a lot of agnostics have no basis for their objective moral values or duties, which is untrue. Why do so many atheists and agnostics manifestly behave morally?

Please read Sam Harris' *The Moral Landscape* to understand how neuroscientists might view the development of moral values.[32]

Per Ylä-Anttila, Jonathan Haidt's moral foundations theory argues that there are certain foundational human capacities for moral cognition, which have evolved via natural selection over millennia.[33, 34]

Craig argues that if morality is just a human convention, then why should we act morally? Well, take My All-Knowing word for it: it is, and you better!

In a speech at Gracepoint Church, Craig offers some further thoughts on the problem of evil and the existence of an All-Good, All-Loving God. Craig states that it is the non-believer who shoulders the burden of proof that evil and suffering, including that from natural disasters, disprove the existence of an All-Powerful, All-Loving God. I would shift the burden of proof too, if I was in Craig's position.

Of course, most non-believers do believe the problem of evil disproves the existence of an All-Powerful, All-Loving God. However, some would agree that the possibility of a God who is not All-Loving, All-Good, and All-Powerful remains. (Hint—You are getting warmer!)

Craig notes the possibility that any world of free persons with as much good as our actual world would also involve as much suffering as our actual world. He concludes that as long as this is even logically possible, it is not necessarily true that God can create just any world that he wants. It seems Craig also believes God is not necessarily All-Powerful.

Lastly, Craig makes the now-standard conjecture supported by no actual evidence, "You see, as finite persons we are limited in intelligence, in insight, in space, and time. But God sees the end of history from the beginning. And he providentially orders history to arrive at his ends through people's free decisions and actions. And in order to arrive at his ultimate ends God may well have to put up with a great deal of suffering along the way. Suffering which appears pointless within our limited framework might be seen to be justly permitted within God's wider framework." [35] I guess that wars, the Holocaust, cancer, children starving, tsunamis, plagues, earthquakes, etc. actually make the world a better place in the long run—just take Craig's word for it. The chances of this are remote, but it is possible, it could be true. What a cop-out.

Apparently, Craig also feels that just "knowing God" is an incommensurable good to which our suffering cannot even be compared. We need to understand that "God's plan for humanity may involve terrible suffering for us, whose point or reason we can't expect to see."[36]

Richard Swinburne, another well-known religious philosopher has weighed in on the reason for natural disasters and diseases. In his opinion, if the only evils were those produced by human beings, we would not have nearly so many opportunities for developing our characters. Natural evils like tsunamis, earthquakes, volcanoes, tornadoes, and diseases allow us opportunities to make choices which we would not ordinarily have. As to how much suffering would outweigh the good of free will, Swinburne notes that at this time, there is not too much evil in the world.[37] Really? Let's have another major earthquake or tsunami, so you can have some good opportunities to impress the Boss!

Lastly, how might Alvin Plantinga, another well-known modern religious philosopher, weigh in on this topic? Plantinga offers his perspective that the perfect love of God requires that he create a world wherein those who suffer are rewarded, so that their lives are better than they would be in worlds where they do not suffer.

Well, how might I do that?

In *Supralapsarianism, or 'O Felix Culpa,'* Plantinga explains that the value of Christ's incarnation and atonement cannot be matched by any amount of creaturely good behavior. No matter how many wonderful people there are, no matter how good their behavior, the value of their lives would not match that of incarnation and atonement; any world with incarnation and atonement would be better yet. No matter how much evil and suffering a world contains, that amount of suffering would be far outweighed by the goodness of Christ's incarnation and atonement. Therefore, any world with incarnation and atonement is of essentially infinite value, no matter how much suffering it contains. Incarnation and atonement were necessary because of sin and evil. Therefore, sin and evil are necessary conditions of the value of every really good possible world.[38] O Felix Culpa indeed!

Alvin Plantinga and others of his ilk make outrageous claims like this and then decry the use of mockery in reaction. He claims that those who think like the self-described "anti-theist" writer Christopher Hitchens, for example, do not propose serious arguments against religious beliefs, instead relying on condescension and mockery.[39]

As explored by Lydia B. Amir in her book *Humor and the Good Life in Modern Philosophy: Shaftesbury, Hamann, Kierkegaard*, according to the well-known seventeenth-to-eighteenth-century philosopher Shaftesbury, "If an opinion cannot stand mockery," then it similarly would be "revealed to be ridiculous."[40]

The use of mockery is a very common complaint of theists and apologists for organized religions who want a serious argument for why it is not rational to believe in an immaterial, unembodied mind (What does that mean?) that has always existed, created our Universe 13.8 billion years ago (How? And from what?), guided our Earth to form roughly 4.5 billion years ago, then life to form and evolve until humans very recently appeared, then started giving out immaterial souls individually designed for humans only (When? What are they for?), maybe sent plagues to Egypt and parted the Red Sea to save his chosen people, or sent his son (who is one of three parts of him) to Earth for thirty-three years, preaching for the last three of them before being crucified for three hours to save all mankind, or sent an angel with a chariot to take a prophet for a heavenly visit, or is one of hundreds or thousands of Gods who assist Southeast Asian people as they cycle between multiple earthly lives. Why would anyone mock these beliefs? Surely spending as much time as possible on arguments either for or against these various depictions of reality is a worthwhile pursuit. Well, maybe if you are a philosopher.

Is there a Supernatural Creator of all things? I am the current God, and I don't know and neither do you. Certainly, if such a being does exist, he is nothing like your organized religions describe.

I have news for you guys—nobody knows Me or what I think. You cannot reason into existence the God you want Me to be. Stop listening to philosophers—especially religious philosophers and apologists with their unavoidable and highly ingrained biases. All that suffering is not to make the human population better in the long run. That idea does not pass the red face test.

My Friend Jack

During a recent sojourn of Mine to planet Earth, an evangelical Christian friend (and a very good person) tried to convince Me that there is an All-Powerful, All-Good God (the Christian one) who would let Me into heaven if I believed in him. Now, since I am God, I tried to be All-Nice and not laugh in My friend's face. I did ask him why an All-Powerful, All-Good God would allow forty-five million children to suffer from malnutrition and over three million children to die from hunger every year. He took his time answering, almost as if he never considered this before. Then he stated that all these children dying was a test from God to see how the rest of humanity responded to this issue. Hmm—this was his concept of an All-Loving, All-Powerful God. This fellow's father was a Protestant preacher, and the power of brainwashing from an early age was on full display.

Clearly, I am not All-Good. And I have a real liking for some pretty pesky microorganisms which I created long before you guys!

Nonetheless, I supposedly listen to all your millions of prayers, forgive your indiscretions, and perform miracles. Just to maintain My mysterious reputation, I prefer to perform these in front of a minimal number of people while no one else is looking. Next year I promise I will let everyone know in advance when and where a good miracle will take place. Maybe in Mumbai where I can guarantee a good, receptive crowd.

Also, I can read your thoughts (Father Riley—knock that off, I am not going to warn you again!), I care about your welfare, I can and will raise you from the dead, etc., etc. Really? Why would I have let all these bad things happen to you guys? Especially the diarrhea and cold sores! Why did I make vegetables taste so bad?

Isn't it obvious to everyone that I screwed up when I created a couple of you guys (Attilla the Hun, Ghengis Khan, Adolf Hitler, Joe "Angel of Death" Mengele, Stalin, Pol Pot, Saddam Hussein, Charles Manson, Idi Amin, Jeffrey Dahmer, Vlad Putin, etc., etc.—not really good role models for your children).

So, I am neither All-Powerful nor All-Good, or I would not let that all happen. I am, however, All-Good Looking. You should see Me in a bathing suit! So, you can forget that "Made in My Image" thing. No way!

Do I Need to be "Perfect"?

Some of you say that, by definition, I have to be eternal, necessary, self-sufficient, unchangeable, All-Powerful, everywhere at once, All-Knowing, infinitely wise and just, All-Good, All-Loving, All-Merciful. I am all these things "perfectly."

Firstly, thanks for saying all these nice things about Me, even though none of you ever met Me, and you know nothing about Me. Who among you has the power or authority to define Me anyway? If you hear someone doing it, you would be wise to immediately leave the room before the lightning strikes. Isn't it "perfectly" obvious that none of the above criteria are necessary for Me to exist? To be your Creator, all I have to be is a lot more knowledgeable and powerful than you. I do not need to be infinitely this or All-That. I do not have to be perfectly anything.

Original Sin and Adam and Eve

This is a fascinating topic for Me. Apparently, many Christians still believe that about six thousand years ago, God created the first human couple, Adam and Eve. They lived in the Garden of Eden where they were forbidden by their Creator to eat "of the tree of knowledge of good and evil . . . for in the day that you eat of it, you shall die." (Gen 2:17).

Well, there was plenty of other food around, so that would have been good enough for Me. But Adam and Eve, tempted by the devil in the form of a snake, disobeyed this commandment. This was man's first sin. All subsequent sins would be disobedience toward God and lack of trust in his goodness.[41]

"By his sin Adam, as the first man, lost the original holiness and justice he had received from God, not only for himself but for all human beings."[42]

Furthermore, "Adam and Eve transmitted to their descendants human nature wounded by their own first sin and hence deprived of original holiness and justice; this deprivation is called 'original sin.'"[43]

Thanks a million, Adam and Eve. In all My glory, I asked you to avoid eating from one tree. There were thousands of other trees around, but like a couple of petulant teenagers, you listened to a slimy snake and ate some special tree fruit anyway. That made Me so mad! For that, I declared all future humans would be born in sin and would experience death. In retrospect, that may have been an overreaction. I realize I can be vengeful sometimes, and I am on some Godly meds to temper that down a bit.

By the way, remember Anselm, that "great" Christian thinker of the eleventh century? Here is how he describes the original sin in his masterwork, *Cur Deus Homo (Why God Became Man)*:

"Man being made holy was placed in paradise, as it were in the place of God, between God and the devil, to conquer the devil by not yielding to his temptation, and so to vindicate the honor of God and put the devil to shame, because that man, though weaker and dwelling upon earth, should not sin, though tempted by the devil, while the devil, though stronger and in heaven, sinned without any to tempt him. And when man could have easily effected this, he, without compulsion and of his own accord, allowed himself to be brought over to the will of the devil, contrary to the will and honor of God." Anselm believed that the number of fallen angels could be replaced in heaven by men taken as substitutes for these fallen angels. Since those bad apples, Adam and Eve, ate the forbidden fruit, Anselm noted ". . . it is not fitting that God should take sinful man without an atonement, in substitution for lost angels; for truth will not suffer man thus to be raised to an equality with holy beings."[44] And Adam was heard to say, "There goes my promotion this year!"

Many modern Christians, realizing that there was no original couple created by God six thousand years ago, and that *Homo sapiens* evolved from other Hominid species, interpret this story as purely mythological or symbolic. In other words, the story of Adam and Eve symbolically describes the fall of mankind into a sinful state. Okay with Me—it is a pretty entertaining fairy tale. Just don't teach it to your children, since it is made-up. Remember—no original parents, no original sin. No original sin, no explanation for sin in the world. No explanation for sin, no need for a savior. Christianity, without the reality of original sin, does not make any sense.

Here's how William Lane Craig, a very bright guy, approaches the existence of Adam in his Reasonable Faith *Defenders* podcast:

"So to deny the historical Adam would be to say that Paul is in theological error in thinking of Adam as a type of Christ. And that threatens to undo Pauline theology. You pull that thread and the whole fabric, I think, threatens to unravel.

Therefore, it does seem to me that there is a lot at stake here and that therefore we should resist, if we can, claims that Adam and Eve were purely symbolic or mythological figures and not historical. So, given the defensibility of Adam and Eve in light of contemporary population genetics and estimations of ancestral population size, I am sticking with the historical Adam and Eve on the basis of Paul's teaching as well as the affirmations in the book of Genesis."[45]

Well, some people will stick with anything, once again confirming the lengths to which religious individuals will go to not change their thinking in the face of new evidence.

In his defense, Craig does not believe original sin is passed to each generation through semen. No original sin genes for him!

Incarnation of Christ

Christian doctrine holds that the Son of Me was a divine being, equal to, but not the same as Me. To save all you sinners, he was incarnated as a human being and was born of a virgin after some hanky-panky by My Holy Spirit. The idea that the Son of Me pre-existed his birth, and that he was a divine being who became human, is found in the Gospel of John (and only in the Gospel of John). "And the Word became flesh and lived among us, and we have seen his glory, the glory as of a father's only son, full of grace and truth." (John 1:14).

Apparently, some people believe the Son of Me was the Word of Me, who coexisted with Me, and was the One through whom the entire universe was created.[46] Well, that's just crazy! No Word or part of Me ever became flesh! Isn't it obvious that some literate, Greek-speaking Christian author wrote this fantasy around the turn of the first century in an attempt to convince his readers that Jesus was divine and Christianity was the one true religion?

Some say the Son of Me had to suffer in human form to save humans from their sinful ways. Our friend Anselm concluded that since all humans are saddled with original sin, no sinful human had the status to make things right with God. So, who could restore what man owes God after a couple of bad apples succumb to Satan's serpentine temptation? This would clearly require a being on the same level as God, but who was also a human. Otherwise, the guilty party—man—does not make the satisfaction. It is necessary that the atoning being would be a perfect God and a perfect man, i.e. a God-man.

Anselm then explains why the Son of Me had to be the one in the Trinity who was born of a virgin. If not Him, then there would be two sons in the Trinity, one Son of God and one Son of a virgin. Of course, the latter would be less noble. Anselm explains further that if the Father became incarnate, there would be two grandsons in the Trinity. The Father would be the grandson of the parents of the virgin, and the Word would be the grandson of the virgin, since he will be the son of her son.[47] So much for the thought process of one of Christianity's greatest thinkers.

And so much for the incarnation. In reality, Jesus was born to a lady named Mary who was married to a carpenter named Joseph. Jesus grew up in a backwater town in Galilee and had several brothers and sisters. He surfaced as an apocalyptic religious preacher and teacher when he was about thirty years old. He preached for a few years before causing a ruckus in a temple in Jerusalem and getting himself arrested for implying he was king of the Jewish people. He was subsequently crucified, leading to his death.

Resurrection and Atonement

Let's talk a bit about this ascending-from-the-dead thing. Just you Christians making trouble again. Look, I did not send the Son of Me to your little rock, so he could waste thirty years (and all those weekly allowances) and then act like a modern-day televangelist for three years, leading up to implicit claims of royalty and some pretty poor behavior in that temple, his subsequent arrest, trial, crucifixion, resurrection, and ascension into heaven, whatever and wherever that is.

For one thing, if My boy ascended into heaven, My Spirit and I would have been there to see that, and I would have arranged for a pretty good crowd to cheer him on. The Son of Me did not rise from the dead. I know it's critical to you, but that's impossible! Nobody saw it, of course. I mean, a crowd at that event would have sealed the deal! Why would I let this happen with no witnesses??? I'm not stupid.

Also—who were these multiple other "saints" that rose from the dead on Crucifiction Day? Funny how that never comes up in church sermons. What else are you Christians hiding? (See Appendix for a few other hidden gems.) According to Matthew 27: 51-57, "And behold, the curtain of the temple was torn in two, from top to bottom. And the earth shook, and the rocks were split. The tombs were also opened. *And many bodies of the saints who had fallen asleep were raised, and coming out of the tombs after his resurrection they went into the holy city and appeared to many.* When the centurion and those who were with him, keeping watch over Jesus, saw the earthquake and what took place, they were filled with awe and said, 'Truly this was the Son of God!'" (Godly italics are Mine.)

Well, truly, a lot of other resurrections were going on that weekend. Maybe these were Daughters of Me, or Stepsons of Me, or Nephews of Me, or Cousins of Me being raised? Why do you think we never hear in church about these "many bodies of the saints" being resurrected and appearing in the holy city?

I think that is obvious. Christian religious leaders want you to think that Christ was the One who was resurrected and appeared to multiple people. That is what makes him God! If many other more ordinary people also were resurrected, that would cloud the message they want you to believe.

Also—these resurrected saints went into the holy city and "appeared to many." If this really happened, it would have made quite a splash in the historical documents written in the region at that time. Of course, it did not. No one seems to know this happened except Matthew. Just like Jesus' resurrection was not recorded concurrently by any non-Christians at the time. Even followers of Christ did not write about the resurrection until years after the event supposedly occurred.

Let's face it, if a person is crucified and the temple curtain tears, many saints' tombs open, followed by the saints' resurrections and appearance to "many" in town, and the resurrected Jesus also appears to five hundred people, wouldn't that at least make the front page of the *Jerusalem News* that week? Headline: "Temple Trouble-Maker and Multiple Saints Rise from the Dead and Appear to Crowds in Jerusalem and Nearby Suburbs!"

Also—according to you guys, the Son of Me left his burial shroud in the tomb. What? He left the tomb naked? Well, no wonder he left in the dark of night. Before he left for good, he appeared (clothed, I might add) to some of his old friends and some strangers. He just appeared with no knock on the door or anything! If the Son of Me can go through solid doors, why did he roll back that stone? That always bothered Me.

Some of you think you have to believe in the Son of Me and his resurrection and ascension in order to get into heaven. I have news for you—if you keep this up, when you physically die, that's it for you. At the least, I will put you in limbo for a few thousand years with no TV, video games, books, or music. You will be begging each other to forget that resurrection/ascension business. That will teach you!

Of course, Christians, Muslims, and some others believe all our dead bodies will be raised from the dead on the Day of Resurrection/Day of Judgment. At that time, we will all be held to account for what we believed and did while we were alive. Of course, I like jazz, so this day will be announced by a trumpet blast. Louis Armstrong will necessarily be raised before everyone else. While I name those folks going to heaven, Louis will play "What a Wonderful World," while those in the "down" elevator will hear a sweet rendition of "Potato Head Blues."

Anyway, the Son of Me spends three hours nailed to a cross wearing a crown of thorns. Is that it? That atones for all the sins of the world since your creation? No way. That was a lot of sins!

How about a few hours in a Brazen Bull? This sixth century BC device was a life-size statue of a bull made of bronze which was heated over a fire until the victim inside was well-done. Now, that would atone for a lot of sins! How about pulling out a few fingernails or spending a day or two on the stretching rack? At least force the Son of Me to read a couple of future Anselm or C.S. Lewis books, or maybe sit through a Catholic mass in Latin without a hymn book to page through.

Faith

My Friend Mike

Mike is another good earthly friend of Mine and a devout Christian. Nothing scares Mike more than a few facts. While sharing lunch one day with some friends, someone mentioned the possibility that there might be more universes out there. Mike's immediate response was, "There are no more universes." Now, I like Mike, but I was pretty sure this investor relations guy was not studying astrophysics on the side. Mike thought more universes would further erode the idea that the Earth and humans are special to his God. Mike would have put Galileo on house arrest in a millisecond. Mike told Me his beliefs were entirely based on faith. He once posted a survey on the internet with two checkboxes:

☐ Facts or ☐ Feelings

That was it, no other words. His position was clear. He had a strong feeling that the Christian God existed and would personally take care of Mike and his family if they believed in and prayed to him—end of discussion. Like many Christians, Mike wears his faith as a badge of honor and avoids all discussions on the topic.

Words such as "firm belief," "trust," "confidence," and "loyalty," are often used to describe what it means to have faith. "Faith" can be applied to individuals (I have faith Sue will do the right thing), natural phenomena (I have faith the Sun will rise tomorrow), processes, and behaviors (I have faith that democracy is the best way of governing). Such uses of the word "faith" are generally based on actual experiences with the subjects (Sue, the Sun, democracy) under discussion. I have to admit that I cringe whenever I hear the word "faith" applied to belief in a Supernatural, Supreme Being.

The Oxford English Dictionary defines faith when applied to religion as a "strong belief in God or in the doctrines of a religion, based on spiritual apprehension rather than proof." In My Godly experience, the words "facts," or "evidence," are rarely associated with discussions of faith in God. Usually, "I have faith," is a phrase you proudly offer when challenged about lack of evidence for your beliefs. There are members of all the religions noted above who claim evidential support for your faith in writings from various two-to-three-thousand-year-old holy books you claim were inspired by Me. Well, the only book I ever inspired is this one. And I never inspired any humans (well, maybe Michelangelo, a little).

Muslims also profess their faith. According to J. Hashmi, Muslims believe that faith consists of three parts: belief in the heart, affirmation by the tongue, and works. Of these, belief in the heart is considered the most important. He claims that it is wrong to say that Islam emphasizes outward actions over inner belief. To Hashmi, no works are accepted by God if one does not hold correct inner belief. Works are only accepted if correct belief is held. Hashmi notes whenever God Almighty mentions works in the Qur'an, the word "belief" precedes it, possibly indicating that belief has more importance in Islam than works.[48]

Well, I have good news for you. You can skip the inane faith, prayer, and worship stuff and just do your share of good works. If you can do this, there is a refurbished rotten body and a nice cottage with the master bedroom on the first floor waiting for you up here!

Christians, Muslims, Jews, and Hindus all have faith that their beliefs are correct. Since tenets of their faiths are incompatible, how can this be okay? Apparently, if you have faith in many Gods and a belief in reincarnation, or one God with three parts who personally takes care of you, or one God who sent an archangel to a cave to tell a prophet what to say and record, or one God who is unknowable but appears as a burning bush, that's okay. But telling the truth by saying "I don't know for sure what is going on here," is not okay? Well, the truth is always okay with Me!

You have such concern for who created you. You are missing the point. I created you. The real important question is who created Me? I am going with an omniscient, All-Powerful, All-Good, All-Loving Creator for Me. That makes Me feel better.

Miracles

In truth, I never really made wine from water. (Although I have probably spent a few thousand hours on that one, and I have not given up yet!) I never got water from a rock, raised people from the dead, cured the blind, made leprosy go away, or leaped tall buildings in a single bound. However, I have pretty quick hands, and if you don't watch closely, I can pull a rabbit out of My headscarf and also sneak some extra loaves and fishes into a breadbasket.

Please stop with the "It's a miracle" nonsense. I am not responsible for winning football, baseball, basketball, hockey, soccer, cricket, or other games. (Although I have fixed a couple Ryder Cup golf matches in My day—USA! USA! USA!) I do not make tornadoes hit some towns and not others. I do not cure some cancers while letting the overwhelming majority of cancer victims die generally slow and painful deaths.

Also, does anyone ever wonder why all the miracles stopped after the invention of recording equipment?

I am pretty good at math and engineering. That Big Bang was a lot of fun for a couple hundred thousand years, but now I have a universe to take care of, and although it's a pretty cool place, it is getting bigger and harder to manage. Who would have thought that some water, organic molecules, and a little lightning would get this whole replication thing going? Four billion years later, you humans are here, and you are not making things any easier. I am thinking about a Big Crunch right now.

How about that dark energy stuff? Now, that is a miracle! Do you think that was easy? I create this whole universe, and at the last minute, I have to come up with some additional energy that does not get diluted as the universe's expansion accelerates. There were not enough candy bars around, so I created dark energy which contributes 70% of the total energy in your universe. This energy keeps the universe from collapsing, so it's kind of important to the whole design. No dark energy, and you are quickly in a very big trash compactor! This was one of My best ideas, and most of you guys have never heard about it. Truthfully, it is pretty confusing, so I kept it out of the Bible. Where would it go, anyway—Genesis maybe—but I was out of days! Okay, okay, in the next edition of the Bible, "On the Eighth Day God created dark energy."

Prayer

You guys pray to Me an awful lot. Since I am All-Good Hearing, sometimes this keeps Me up at night. You ask Me for all kinds of stuff. When something happens that you like, you say I answered your prayers, and it is a gift from Me. When you don't like something, it is not My fault. Hey, I am All-Faultless! Apparently, I can make tornadoes miss your towns (How about the ones they hit?), I can make your sporting team win (How about the 50% of teams that lose?), and I can make you successful in your job (How about those who are not successful?). I can cure your diseases if I want. I know it feels good to think a God influenced your life for the better, but please, take about three seconds to contemplate what you are saying. Anyway, I want some credit for the bad things, too. They take some effort!

And please, please, I beg you—stop sending "thoughts and prayers," and I mean forever! How about "thoughts and get off your butt and do something." That would show some real initiative.

And stop saying "God Knows," "God Bless You," and "Thank God," (usually when a tornado hits someone else's trailer). Why would I bless you when you sneeze? Just cover your nose and mouth when you do it. I am going to cut out all sneezing down there unless I hear a *"Gesundheit!"* every so often.

Lastly, no more saying "Have a blessed day." Ask the kids over in Gaza how many blessed days I am giving out.

Worship

No worship—stop with the worship! Even if I exist and am All-Powerful, All-Good, All-Loving, and All-Knowing, I am definitely not worthy of worship. No being is worthy of worship. What does worthy of worship mean, anyway? You do not exist to glorify Me. I would smite Myself if I made that your purpose. That worship idea came from religious leaders who want to pack their churches, mosques, temples, and offering plates as much and as often as possible. Just take care of your families and neighbors and treat everyone the way you want them to treat you. That's it. I don't want worship. It smacks of brainwashing and cultism. I do not want you kneeling down or prostrating yourself on a rug while you pray to Me. That is the opposite of what I want. I practice humility. I am not taking notes on who worships Me. That would make Me All-Narcissistic and a terrible God. You look stupid spending hours every Saturday, Sunday, or even weekdays worshiping Me instead of eating your favorite breakfast with your kids. And praying to Me five times a day is not necessary. Get your work done, then go home, and have dinner with your family.

News Flash—no credit if you do stuff just for Me!

Weekend socializing is okay (and often fun)—just meet and converse, or go build shelters for the homeless, or do something else you like. Stop using Me as your excuse to get dressed up and spend time with your friends.

Okay, I just decided—I am going to punish anyone who worships Me. When you get up here, I am going to make you attend Catholic Mass in Latin for eight hours a day (yes, we have days). This could be especially tough for you non-Catholics, but you brought it on yourselves. While I am on it—stop with the catechism, the religious madrasas, the Bible schools, Jewish traditions and schools, praying five times a day, etc., etc. Why do you torture your children so?

Let them enjoy childhood and discuss God and religion when they are old enough to understand and think about such topics. Did you ever wonder why kids with Christian parents become Christians, kids with Muslim parents become Muslims, kids with Jewish parents become Jews, kids with Hindu parents become Hindus, kids with Buddhist parents become Buddhists, etc., etc.????

Of course you have, and you know why this happens, so let's not spend a lot of time on this one (not something you like to ponder anyway, as an inconvenient truth emerges immediately). You should know that I am taking points off for all you parents who have considered this and still teach your young children your own brand of religion anyway.

Let's be honest—you are trying to brainwash them before they can understand and freely consider what you are saying.

Souls

You guys talk about "souls" all the time without the faintest clue what you are talking about. I guess you can see that the body just rots away after you die. That is kind of incompatible with an afterlife, so to keep you from getting too depressed you invent an individual and immortal soul. This soul is the spiritual part of you, and I allegedly created this soul for you at, or near, the time of your conception. Your soul is immaterial and invisible and departs from your body after you die. Somehow, this immaterial soul, which never hurt anybody but has marks on it anyway, gets judged and ends up in a good place or a bad place for eternity. A lot of you think that on Judgment Day, the soul is reunited with your previously rotten body and gets a thumbs-up or a thumbs-down. Now, suppose you were saddled with an ugly body during your time on Earth. (Let's face it, most of you are not that attractive.) What kind of God would reunite your soul for eternity with a body you did not want? Who wants to be ugly in heaven? To get around this, some believers have decided that you get a better body when you are resurrected—maybe a young George Clooney or Jane Fonda look.

Many mind-body dualists believe the mind is, or is part of, your soul. The soul is immaterial, and each soul is assigned to each individual sometime after conception. Are all these souls the same or different when assigned? Your non-physical soul inter-acts with just your brain to create your thoughts and actions.

Right away, I have a couple questions for you mind/body dualists.

Firstly, if the soul is non-physical, what is it exactly? No one ever says what it is, only what it is not. How does your non-physical soul causally interact with your physical brain? In other words, if one believes, as Craig does, that matter is made out of one kind of stuff, and the soul or mind is made out of a fundamentally different non-physical stuff, it is not obvious to this God what it means to say that the two interact.

William Lane Craig is not afraid to tell you what a soul is. In his Question of the Week Q&A #479: "What Does it Mean to Say God Is a Soul?" he states, "By a soul, I mean a living, spiritual substance. In characterizing God as a soul, I mean what Jesus meant when he said, 'God is spirit' (John 4.24). A human soul *has* rational cognitive faculties but is not *identical* with its rational faculties, since faculties are not something that exist on their own in abstraction from the thing that has them. What is a soul? It's what you are without your body." Well, that clears things up!

Craig goes on to propose that we think of God "as a soul endowed with three sets of rational faculties, each sufficient for personhood, so that God is tri-personal . . . *What exactly is this nebulous 'thing' that unifies . . . these persons?* It is the spiritual substance whose faculties they are. It is the immaterial entity or being which has these faculties."

Faculties are your physical and mental abilities. So, it seems God has one soul and three sets of physical and mental abilities. [49] Hey, that's a Trinity! Of course, there is no explanation for how an immaterial God has physical abilities, including the ability to create and interact with matter. That is inexplicable.

As for children who have died without baptism, the Catholic Church can only entrust their souls to the mercy of God. "All the more urgent is the Church's call not to prevent little children coming to Christ through the gift of holy baptism."[50]

Under natural conditions, embryo loss is approximately 10-40% before implantation in the uterus, and total loss from fertilization to birth is 40-60%.[51] As previously noted, about 120 billion humans have been born. If conception comes with a free soul, and half the embryos never make it, that makes about 120 billion more human souls I have to take care of. So, what happens to these souls? On Judgment Day are they reunited with their physical embryos? I have to be upfront with you. I accidentally threw a few billion of those embryos out one day because the smell was so terrible. Don't worry, I have an idea for cloning some pretty attractive bodies to reunite the unpaired souls with.

Another large number of you think something entirely different happens to your soul. According to the Hindu Vedas, all beings are souls and thus spiritual in nature. Though the body is temporary and eventually dies, the soul is eternal. The soul is uplifted through every good action performed and degraded with every bad action. After death, the soul is reincarnated, taking birth in another physical body, where it continues on a journey of spiritual development.[52]

If this sounds outrageous and fabricated out of whole cloth to you, congratulations—your brain is working and maybe you will get into heaven (maybe). As for the rest of you, I can't have a lot of magical thinking in heaven. It leads to cultism and conspiracy theories, so it may be limbo for you.

And when did I draw the line on giving out souls? Apparently, you think only recently evolved humans have a material body and an immaterial soul/spirit? Why just humans and why just recently evolved ones?

Richard Dawkins notes that every creature ever born belonged to the same species as its parents. The process of evolution is so gradual that we can never say "Now we have the first human!" It was always a case of just slightly different from the previous generation. Per Dawkins, "That's a scientific point which I think is quite interesting. I'm not sure if it has a theological significance except that I think successive popes have tried to suggest that the soul did indeed get added, rather like gin to tonic, at some particular point during evolution."[53]

J.P. Moreland notes in *The Soul: How We Know It's Real and Why It Matters* that all animals do have souls, but non-human animal souls are not as richly structured as ours, and, of course, do not bear the image of God as humans do. Lastly, the non-human animal souls are more dependent on the animal's body and sense organs.[54]

So, non-human animals may also have non-physical souls that interact mysteriously with their brains to create their physical and mental abilities. I am not sure what happens when a hyena pack kills a zebra to feed themselves and their families, but I understand we are running out of magic soul markers in the heavenly supply store.

What does getting a soul mean anyway? Let Me ask again, "What's a soul?" If I put five people in five separate rooms and asked them what a soul is (or what God is for that matter), how many descriptions do you think I would get? I tried it once and got twenty-six! One idea I considered was that every time a bell rings, a human gets a soul. Unfortunately, someone else came up with a similar idea first, so, ethically, I could not use that one.

Catholicism teaches that:[55]

"The soul refers to the innermost aspect of man, that which is of greatest value in him, that by which he is most especially in God's image: 'soul' signifies the *spiritual principle* in man."

"The human body shares in the dignity of 'the image of God': it is a human body precisely because it is animated by a spiritual soul . . ." (What???)

"The unity of soul and body is so profound that one has to consider the soul to be the 'form' of the body: i.e., it is because of its spiritual soul that the body made of matter becomes a living, human body." Hey, I think I read that in one of your college freshman biology books.

"The [Catholic] Church teaches that every spiritual soul is created immediately by God—it is not produced by the parents—and also that it is immortal: it does not perish when it separates from the body at death, and it will be reunited with the body at the final Resurrection."

Where are all those souls stored before they are assigned to individual creatures? Do they require refrigeration? Luckily, they are immaterial, so you can get a lot of them in a small space.

Anyway, if I had some souls to give out, every creature would have gotten one, and they all would have gotten a shot at heaven. Not hell, though. I would never send a dog or cat to hell. That option is reserved just for you guys.

Grace

"Gracious means to be considerate, to show favor. That God is gracious would mean that he is favorably inclined toward us. That he wants to show favor to us. To do what is best for us."[56]

"Grace is *favor, the free and undeserved help* that God gives us to respond to His call to become children of God, adoptive sons, partakers of the divine nature and of eternal life."[57]

"Grace is a *participation in the life of God.* It introduces us into the intimacy of Trinitarian life: by Baptism the Christian participates in the Grace of Christ, the Head of his Body. As an 'adopted son,' he can thenceforth call God 'Father' in union with the only Son. He receives the life of the Spirit who breathes charity into him and who forms the Church."[58]

"Since it belongs to the supernatural order, grace *escapes our experience* and cannot be known except by faith."[59]

So, Christians think grace is favor shown to humans by a Supernatural Being like Me. You don't deserve it, but I give it to you anyway.

The Holy Trinity

There is no Trinity up here as most of you know. Who came up with that one anyway? Those Christians again—what a knife in My side. (Hey, that's a good one!) I am still waiting for a good explanation of this three-in-one God thing. How does that work anyway—I might try it if someone can help Me. Then I could send the Son of Me or the Spirit of Me off to suffer and make up for your sins without any pain on My end. That works for Me, so send Me an e-mail with the details. That's godinheaven@fabrication.com.

Even the Son of Me did not believe in a Trinity of equals. (John 14:28, "The Father is greater than I am.") How does a force, pure love, or an unembodied mind have a son, anyway? As far as I know, it's just Me trying to control a billion evil spirits attempting to kill you every day. (Haha, I am just messing with you.)

So, who actually created this doctrine, and when? Rebecca Denova, Emeritus Professor of Early Christianity in the Department of Religious Studies at the University of Pittsburgh, notes that around 325 CE, Christian communities were heatedly debating the relationship between Jesus and the God of Israel. The Roman Emperor, Constantine, called for an ecumenical meeting at Nicaea in modern-day Turkey to settle the issue. This was the First Council of Nicaea. The Council decided that the God of Israel was the greatest God but now was to be worshiped simultaneously with Jesus as the identical essence of God, along with the spirit of God (the Holy Spirit). Thus, the concept of the Holy Trinity was born.[60]

That's right, the Holy Trinity was made up out of whole cloth about three hundred years after Christ died. In addition, this First Council also settled the question of whether Jesus Christ was divine and what his relationship was to God the Father. Again, these items were decided by church fathers three hundred years after the death of Christ. Another output of this meeting was the original Nicene Creed. Later amended, this creed was a statement of belief for all Christians (See Appendix).

The Virgin Birth

For you Christians, there is no such thing as the Holy Spirit part of Me impregnating a woman who goes on to have a virgin birth. That story is a classic up here! Women out there who have been impregnated by someone other than your husband—have you ever tried the virgin birth explanation? How did that go? And how about Joseph, how do you think this makes him feel? He meets a sweet young lady, gets married, has the Son of God for a kid, and gets no credit!! He gets very little mention in the Bible. You don't even know if this guy could cut a true right angle for My sake. FYI, he was a great carpenter with a specialty in aqueduct infrastructure and a sub-specialty in crucifixes, of all things.

This virgin birth thing has Me wondering how the Son of Me got forty-six chromosomes, including a "Y" male chromosome.

Anyway, just to be sure, I sent some Son of Me saliva to a genealogy company, and they confirmed that the Son of Me had forty-six chromosomes, including the "Y" chromosome. So, unless the Holy Spirit is a male capable of passing along half of his forty-six chromosomes, I am going with Joseph as the Son of Me's father.

Mary Magdalene

Now there was a good-looking woman! I just had to give her a shoutout. Mary M. and the Son of Me were a couple up until Crucifixion Weekend. She was a really nice lady, and she was always there for him. I wish I had given her more play in the Bible books I inspired. She helped a lot with the "Sermon on the Mount" talk, which put the Son of Me on the map, so to speak. To reward her, the Son of Me appeared to her first on the Sunday morning after the crucifixion. Always joking around, the Son of Me surprised her and almost gave her a heart attack! The Son of Me said to her, "Mary." She turned and said to him in Hebrew, "Rabboni!" (John 20:16-17). Well, he was naked. As a parting gift, the Son of Me gave Mary his crown of thorns as a keepsake.

Angels and Holy Spirits

Angels are everywhere! They are spirits, but they can talk. The archangels in particular deliver important messages to Christians and Muslims alike. For example, "The Holy Ghost is arranging for you to bear a child who will be the Son of God/the Messiah," or, "O Muhammad, you are the messenger of God, and I am the angel Jibril (Gabriel)." This latter revelation was followed by others about the one true God. The angel also told Muhammad to begin proclaiming God's message.

There are also guardian angels for everyone.

". . . the whole life of the [Catholic] Church benefits from the mysterious and powerful help of angels. From its beginning until death, human life is surrounded by their watchful care and intercession. Beside each believer stands an angel as protector and shepherd leading him to life. Already here on Earth, the Christian life shares by faith in the blessed company of angels and men united in God."[61]

I feel obligated to say a word or two about that very bad angel, Satan. For insight into the Christian version see a lesson on "The Origin of Satan," as recorded in William Lane Craig's "Doctrine of Creation," Part 22, in 2018 and found on his very extensive and well-organized website, Reasonable Faith. Craig laments that the Bible does not explicitly address how God created something like Satan that seems to be so intrinsically evil and opposed to God. Craig notes that we have evidence in Scripture specifically of sin on the part of Satan which would bring him into condemnation before God.

Craig further notes that the traditional understanding of Satan and the demons is very plausible. This involves God creating a realm of good angels who, using their free will, rebelled against God and were condemned. So, the Earth lies somewhat under the power of these demonic angels. Craig notes that some of these fallen angels become what we would call demons.[62]

American Muslim scholars note that Satan, "Shaytan" in Arabic, is believed to be a third type of creation, in addition to humans and angels known as "jinn." Humans are said to have been made from clay, angels from light, and *jinn* from fire. While the Qur'an teaches that some *jinn* are good and submit to God, it states that others, such as Iblis or Shaytan (Satan), try to tempt people to do evil, similar to the belief about Satan in traditional Christian theology.[63]

How about the Holy Spirit? The Christians really got it right this time. Per the Roman Catholic Catechism, the Holy Spirit is, "The third divine Person of the Blessed Trinity, the personal love of Father and Son for each other. Also called the Paraclete (Advocate) and Spirit of the Truth, the Holy Spirit is at work with the Father and the Son from the beginning to the completion of the divine plan for our Salvation."[64]

Huh? Some parakeet represents the love for each other of the two other parts of God? Somehow this love gets up, shaves, and goes to work on a divine plan every day. Anyone ever see this plan, or at least a concept for this plan? Let's be honest, nobody could believe this without some very professional, early childhood brainwashing.

The Eucharist

The word "Eucharist" refers to the Sacrament of the Eucharist, which is the belief that at some Christian services (especially Catholic mass), the body and blood of Jesus Christ are truly represented on the altar by bread and wine after transubstantiation by the priest.

This belief derives from the Last Supper when the Son of Me and his disciples were eating and joking around a little. The Son of Me took a loaf of bread, and after blessing it, he broke it, gave it to the disciples, and said, "Take, eat; this is my body." Then he took a cup, and after giving thanks he gave it to them, saying, "Drink from it, all of you; for this is my blood of the covenant, which is poured out for many for the forgiveness of sins" (Matthew 26: 26-28).

Now, I should tell you that Son of Me was quite a joker and was definitely spoofing these guys. Thomas was rolling his eyes, but the rest of them believed it, and now every Sunday priests get to drink a cup of wine with a little sourdough wafer on the side. The brainwashing parents get to line up their hungry little ones to get a wafer, too. Who would pass up a chance to have a Son of God snack for breakfast?

Let's be honest. If, outside a church environment, a friend of yours told you he had changed a piece of bread and some wine into the body and blood of someone who lived two thousand years ago, you would consider him a lunatic. That is good thinking.

Heaven

Let's talk about this heaven thing that you invented to keep everyone hopeful and believing in your particular religion, no matter how crazy it sounds. Where is heaven, and what does heaven look like? Why do you always point up when you talk about heaven? Do you know something I don't know?

One thing you got right—there is a gatekeeper.

It is not Peter. He was not really very good with the books—not a great fisherman either, as I recall. But he was generally a true and mostly loyal friend, although every time I hear a cock crow up here, I am reminded of his actions on a very bad weekend the Son of Me had back in March/April of his thirty-third year. While I am thinking of it, I am banning any more cocks from entering heaven—they can find their own paradise. And that Judas, he made a little money, but was it really worth it? You see, I made him the gatekeeper, so while everyone else is having a little heavenly fun, Judas has to listen to all those excuses from schmucks who don't really belong here. Serves him right.

Is there a heaven, and is it really a paradise? Hmmm—I would not call it a paradise, but if you would rather not be dead and gone, it makes a pretty good alternative. Nobody works here, and it is generally a pretty happy place.

Heaven is certainly not like you guys always describe after your end-of-life experiences, which makes Me think you are just making up more nonsense. After you die, you will not see a bright light of any kind (unless you are taken to the interrogation room, in which case your goose is cooked anyway). You will not fly, and you will not see relatives all dressed up in earthly clothes and anxious to talk with you. Nobody wears clothes in heaven—why would they? It is sort of a nudist colony for souls. Sunny and eighty degrees every day.

Everyone has a nice ranch home or sometimes a three-bedroom colonial with a master suite on the first floor! Nobody has to work, but there is a lot of volunteering. Golf and shuffleboard are very popular, and the pool and library are always full.

Now, pay attention—there are lots of other earthly creatures here. If I were you, I would stay away from the cow and chicken areas. They have long memories, and they especially love filet of soul. Also, there is a dinosaur pavilion that you should avoid. They like to sprinkle humans over their food. Just avoid the parts of heaven where the firmament is shaking.

Where is heaven and how will physical bodies live there if it is a spiritual place? You got Me there, so let's just skip that question.

Hell, Purgatory, and Limbo

There is no eternal damnation, so let's skip over that one, too. Why would I create a creature, let it live in a human body for a short period of time, and then burn it for eternity because it did not meet my standards? No All-Good, All-Loving God I know would do that, that's for sure. Some Christians believe that, even if you lived an otherwise exemplary life, you must believe in the Christian God, or you go to hell for eternity. Naturally, the 1.4 billion Hindus in the world are opposed to this line of thinking.

Partial burning in purgatory is okay with Me for those with extra marks on their souls. I favor walking on hot coals or putting out candles with your fingertips. Nothing too dramatic. Once I burn most of those extra marks off your soul, you get in. How do you feel about fourteen billion years being a short time for Me now?

As for limbo, the name is so cool that it has to exist whether it makes sense or not. It is a place for unbaptized Christian babies and some adults who are still saddled with original sin. For Muslims, it might be the state after death and before the final Judgment Day. I know for a fact that the real limbo has music and these bars that people dance under as the bars are slowly lowered.

Space and Time

You say I am outside space and time, but I can alter space and time—which is it? Stop saying crazy stuff with absolutely no supporting data. Here's a heads-up. If you say I am outside space and time again, you will find out what pure energy feels like! I am not outside space and time. What does that mean, anyway? Where does space end?

Space and time are very connected. You guys should listen to Sean Carroll who notes that in the old days we thought that space was static, and that time just flowed from past to future. If Newton had been correct, time and space would have been separate. Then Einstein comes along and realizes that space and time are connected, and that space-time can change. It can be warped or curved. You experience that curvature as gravity, so you know it's there.[65]

Anyway, I am intimately involved with and interact with you and your universe. I created your universe, the Milky Way, the Sun, Earth, and you. I care personally for you and will raise you from the dead and deliver you into heaven, if you believe in Me and love Me. A little worship here and there wouldn't hurt your chances (I kid, I kid).

Some say I existed outside of time before I created your universe, but after the creation, I entered a temporal state. Nice try, all you humans dealing with Me being eternal. Believe Me, there was time before your universe was created. So much that even I can't remember how everything started. However, I am convinced My Creator knows what happened. He left Me some notes somewhere. They are in My "Creation of the Universe" folder. I will search My heavenly files just before Judgment Day and, if I can understand what's in there, I will let you know how it all started.

The Unembodied Mind

Most believers probably never heard this one, but a number of philosophers have determined that due to a lot of requirements for him/her/them to have existed, your God likely exists in the form of an unembodied mind. You see, religious philosophers often claim that I cannot be a physical entity because all matter has a creator. If I was material, I could not be God. This unembodied mind is a personal agent who must be timeless, non-spatial, immaterial, intelligent, and powerful.[66]

Jason Dulle further notes that there is nothing logically incoherent about a disembodied mind. (What??) He says our minds cause things to happen, and he sees no reason to think this capacity is dependent on your mind being embodied. He states based on zero evidence that your minds are immaterial. The immaterial mind is an old argument as demonstrated by examining correspondence between René Descartes (1596-1650) and Princess Elisabeth of Bohemia, whom he tutored. Descartes believed in the dualism of the mind and body.

The Princess writes:

" . . . tell me how the soul of a human being (it being only a thinking substance) can determine the bodily spirits, in order to bring about bodily actions. For it seems all determination of movement happens through the impulsion of the thing moved, by the manner in which it is pushed by that which moves it, or else by the particular qualities and shape of the latter. Physical contact is required for the first two conditions, extension for the third. You entirely exclude the one [extension] from the notion you have of the soul, and the other [physical contact] appears to me incompatible with an immaterial thing."

Elisabeth is asking, how could a non-physical mind move matter? For one object to move another requires them to be in physical contact, or at least requires one object to have a surface to do the pushing. Elisabeth denies that a non-physical mind without a location in space could possibly affect a physical body. Why not take the mind to be physical, instead? Today, most philosophers and scientists see no strong reason, in principle, why behavior cannot be explained in physical terms.[67]

Dulle neglects to mention that your minds only act causally on your own bodies, which suggests, at least to this God, that your mind is a part of you, likely located in your brain case, and capable of making you have thoughts and feelings and moving your body parts through neural connections with other parts of your brain, including your motor cortex.

Time and a lot of further research will tell. Let's face it, departments of neuroscience have existed for about sixty years. I gave the dinosaurs 165 million years on Earth. Let's give neuroscientists another thousand more years before we decide our minds are immaterial. (Hint: they are not.)

By that time your brains will be supplemented with digital computing power through connections to the Cloud that will let you analyze data and form thoughts incredibly faster. I hope your immaterial souls can keep up!

Clergy, Holy People, and Some Religious Behaviors

How about the brainwashers-in-chief: the reverends, priests, rabbis, imams, monks, other holy leaders, and their support staff? Bunch of freeloaders, if you ask Me.

Also, you Catholic priests have to be men and cannot get married! (I was mad at Catholics the day I came up with that one.) As an aside, would a truly perfect God allow pedophiles to assume a large role in churches?

And you nuns also cannot get married. You have to wait on the priests like servants and wear the most uncomfortable outfits I could come up with. I had just come back from Antarctica when I came up with the design.

And stop with the infallibility of the pope in religious matters—I can tell you, at best he deserves a "B" grade in such matters, and most recently one of these guys almost got a failing grade in an opinion on the Religious Ramifications of Existentialism (admittedly a tough subject even for Me).

By the way, I insist all you religious people wear hats, grow beards, get funny haircuts, eat fish on certain days, don't eat pork or beef, fast for periods of time, don't cook on certain days, hide women behind veils, pray multiple times a day facing in a particular direction, go to churches on particular days of the week, eat pieces of stale bread that have been converted to

Me, put ashes on your foreheads, carry prayer beads, etc., etc. (Not!!!!!)

Also—I hereby declare that all men can shake hands with women to whom they are not married. And you can say My name and paint or sculpt representations of Me, even if you don't have a clue what I look like. Please stop with the holy undergarments. That is a little too weird even for Me.

And let's stop fighting wars over who succeeds a fake prophet or governs a holy city in Israel, for Pete's sake. Speaking of Peter, or "The Rock," as we called him (a really bad swimmer who would often "sink like a rock" in the Sea of Galilee). What a traitor! Denies the Son of Me three times and then sneaks off back to the fishing boat. Well, truthfully, he stuck with the Son of Me for quite a while before and after that infamous weekend, so I made him My go-to guy despite these transgressions.

In summary—all you holy people, please get a real job! If you want to be nice to the downtrodden, that is great! Just do it in your spare time and get others to help you if you can.

Divine Succession

The Prophet Muhammad was succeeded by twelve distinguished successors from the line of Muhammad. These successors are called imams, and according to Shia Muslims, they were appointed by God. Shia Muslims believe the right to ordain imams belongs to God.[68]

Shia Muslims believe that the Prophet Muhammad's successor should be from Muhammad's bloodline. Sunni Muslims believe that the Prophet did not explicitly declare a successor, and that a suitably holy man, not necessarily from Muhammad's bloodline, could attain this position. Therefore, Sunnis are opposed to political succession based on Muhammad's bloodline.[69]

Because of the disagreement on this major issue, Shia and Sunni Muslims have been in conflict (sometimes violent) for over fourteen hundred years.

Divine succession? There is no divine succession. Just elect the best people you can and stop fighting about this, or I am going to allow your women to take off their headscarves and wear shorts when it gets hot outside. And those peepholes are going to get bigger.

Monotheism vs. Polytheism

Are there other Gods or just Me? That's a tough question. Over a billion Hindus believe there are many Gods. However, if you say there is more than one God to a Muslim, you might not make it to dinner that night. Most Christians believe there is one God, but they cheat and say that one God has three separate but equal parts. Many religions profess that God is unknowable (good answer—and true!), but then they go on to tell you a lot about Me anyway. Based on My experience, I lean towards just Me, but how would I know? Oh, I forgot—I am omniscient.

When the time comes, what should I tell the billions of polytheists in the world, many of whom have never even heard of Me, and therefore could not believe in Me and get into heaven? That they were just unlucky to be born in Asia? That I have no real data for their beliefs? Don't laugh, the same holds for you monotheist guys.

In his book, *Mere Christianity*, the esteemed Christian apologist C.S. Lewis addressed the question of outcomes for those who never heard of the Christian God. He notes that the outcomes for such individuals used to puzzle him. He felt it was unfair to exclude from heaven people who had never heard of Jesus Christ and, thus, had not been able to believe in him. Since God has not explicitly told us what happens to such individuals, Lewis concludes we actually do not know that only those who know Christ can be saved through Him.[70] (Good thinking, Mr. Lewis)

That is Lewis' long-winded way of saying, "Good question, I don't know the answer, but I am not going to think about it anymore."

On this same issue, William Lane Craig notes there are a couple of levels to consider:[71]

Firstly, God judges people on the basis of the knowledge they possess. Craig proposes that those who have never heard of Christ will not be judged according to whether they have believed in Christ. He feels it may be that God will judge these people based on their response to God's general revelation in nature and in conscience. If they express the appropriate response, Christ's death on the cross may also lead to their salvation.

Craig also notes that God may have ordered the world so that anyone who would respond to the Gospel if he heard it is born at a time and place in history where he does hear it. In this way, no one is lost through accidents of geography and history.

This is ridiculous, of course. It asserts that people born in areas without knowledge of Christ were purposely born there because they were never going to believe anyway. Nice of Me!

Lastly, Craig suggests to his evangelical audience that God knows that you will be sharing the Gospel with others and has arranged divine appointments for you. According to Craig, God may place persons who he knows would respond to the Word of God into various groups that evangelists can reach. So, there may well be such divine appointments out there waiting for his audience members. To Dr. Craig, this gives tremendous incentive to the task of world evangelization.

Me (God): This is the point where we all take a deep breath and agree with each other that religious apologists and philosophers can and will come up with totally irrational reasoning to support any position they want, even if there are people nearby checking the straps on a straitjacket just their size.

Anyway, maybe there is a God for each universe, and maybe a couple Gods. I wonder if parts of them had to suffer physical pain for three hours to save their higher-functioning creatures. Maybe I will try a wormhole adventure to find out.

Creation of You and Your Universe?

Why Did I Do It?

That's an excellent question! Sometimes I wish I hadn't, but then there would be no NFL on Sundays! Was I just bored? Did I just feel creative that day?

By the way—it is okay to say, "I don't know." That has the advantage of being true and beats the hell out of fabricating a story such as this: a woman was informed by an angel that she was to be made pregnant by a Holy Spirit of Me and give virgin birth to a Son of Me. The Son of Me then grew up as the stepson of a carpenter and roughly thirty years later became a holy preacher who promoted good behavior before he trashed a Jerusalem temple in a fit of rage, let people call him King of the Jews, and was crucified as punishment in order to forgive all our sins. He then rose from the dead and appeared to a few folks before rejoining himself in heaven to return on a date to be named later to resurrect and pass judgment on everyone.

Much more likely, My Creator (or maybe his Creator) decided that I needed a little company, some creatures that I could love, imbue with a soul, and reward in an afterlife if they believe in Me and worship Me. Anyway, making all your rotten bodies rise from the dead all at once will be the best parlor trick ever. I can't wait.

After spending an eternity outside or inside of space and time, why would I wait fourteen billion years for you guys to arrive on a very tiny little rock nowhere special in, for you, an unimaginably large universe? And don't tell Me that maybe fourteen billion years is just seconds to an entity like Me. That's ridiculous! If this were true, it would mean your time on Earth is so short as to be meaningless to Me. Well, time does fly.

How does that work anyway? If I have been here for eternity, that means I have been here forever, going backward. None of what you see could ever be here because the past would be infinite, and we would never get to the present! Oh, I forgot—time did not exist before the Big Bang. Wrong!

Remember, there are two hundred billion or more stars per galaxy and over two hundred billion galaxies in your universe. That is over 10,000,000,000,000,000,000,000 stars out there with lots and lots of planets going around them. The closest star to you in your galaxy is 4.3 light years away. (That means light from that star traveling 186,000 miles per second takes over four years to get here.) A little easy multiplication tells you the closest star to you is about twenty-five trillion miles away. By the way, I am really good at math, although Linear Algebra always gave Me a problem.

As I said, your planet is a rock twenty-five thousand miles around and eight thousand miles in diameter. That is very, very small and insignificant in the grand scheme of things. Your planet has a little water on top, a nifty little atmosphere (You are welcome!), and some pretty good landscaping, if I do say so Myself.

Your Christian Bible says I made all this in six days and then rested. Well, I am telling you it took a lot longer than that, and I still came in on time and on budget!

You were easy to make—just squeeze together a lot of elementary particles, give it a little time (yes, there was time outside of your universe then), and—*presto-chango!*—you get a Big Bang, inflation, expansion of the universe at different rates, contraction of more dense regions of the universe, and galaxy, star, and planet formation. About 4.5 billion years ago, I allowed Earth to form, and a while later, evolution to occur. Now there is all kinds of life in the universe, including you. But who made Me—and why do you avoid this greatest question of all?

I did take a big rest after I was done—much longer than one day. I have a preference for the beach, so I went for about a month to My oceanfront home on a distant planet from you, reread Richard Dawkins' *The God Delusion* (one of My favorites), and then—back to work! Gotta keep all My new creations humming along!

Fairness and Equality

Some of My creatures are born to starving families in every region of the world including the United States, Asia, Africa, South America, and others, instead of being born to a wealthy or even properly middle-class family somewhere else. Who thinks that is fair? What All-Loving God would do that? Everyone is not "born equal," and not everybody is born with the same rights and opportunities in the Americas, Europe, Africa, Asia, or anywhere else! Isn't that obvious? Even to you old-money Republicans? This is not rocket science, and this time, it *is* a test for the rest of you.

By the way—I apologize to all you poor people. I just have trouble dialing in all the fairness correctly—but I am working on it. Maybe that Planck constant is a little off or something. Anyway, I will try to make it up to you later. The meek shall inherit the Earth, or something like that.

Evolution

Evolution is a fact (and one of My best ideas ever). Populations evolve due to genetic changes accumulated from one generation to the next. There is continuous, non-random natural selection of populations that have a genetic makeup more compatible with survival in their environment.

So, your big ears, funny noses, body smells, and maybe even your religious proclivities have come about because in ways, some more obvious than others, they promote your survival and therefore the survival of the genes you carry.

In 2011, Mora et al, estimated there are approximately 8.7 million species of plants and animals on Earth.[72] Other estimates are over 10 million. Of course, many, many more species have gone extinct over the past three to four billion years. This should serve as a reminder that this is not just about you. If it was, I would have created you first and not bothered with billions of years of evolution and a lot of wasted effort on My part.

Judgment Day

Most religions have their own version of how this is all going to end.

In Christianity, the Bible's Book of Revelation details Armageddon, the final battle on Earth between the forces of Good and Evil (God and Satan). If you have never read this final book of the New Testament, I would encourage you to do so. Nobody has ever, ever put pen to paper and come up with anything crazier than the Book of Revelation. Anyone who says My Holy Spirit inspired this book will be banished for all time to the Judgment Day section of the heavenly library with Books of Revelation to read and Bruce Willis Armageddon DVDs to watch—that's it!

Many Hindus claim that Vishnu will return to Earth and battle evil while riding on a white horse carrying a sword that looks like a comet.

In Islam, the end of the world is referred to as the Hour. This involves Jesus slaying the anti-Christ who has put the planet in peril. This is followed by a period of harmony, then Jesus' death, followed by a time of destruction leading to the Hour when souls. . .[73]

Okay—more fiction from your religious leaders. Just hang in there. In a little bit, I will tell you all you need to know about My plans for Judgment Day.

The "Just in Case" Case

Very briefly—and I have heard this one a million times—"It does not take up that much of my time to profess belief, go to church, and pray to my God. If there is a God, heaven, and hell, I am covered for eternity. If not, I just wasted a little time."

Anybody who has practiced that philosophy—you are going to waste a little more time in purgatory where you will be in charge of the charcoal briquets.

In *Philosophers On God: Talking about Existence,* Daniel J. Hill talks about Pascal's wager in his chapter "Why God Matters" (using the analogy of a game of Russian roulette): "What do you stand to *lose* if God exists, and you don't care or don't believe?

Well, according to the Western monotheists, you run the risk of everlasting punishment in hell. The conclusion of Pascal's wager is this: whether God exists or not, it doesn't make sense for us not to believe . . . betting against the existence of God would be like betting that the gun with three loaded chambers won't kill you. You have very little to gain, but—as one might put it—a hell of a lot to lose."[74] Well, to this God, Pascal's wager sounds like an appeal based on fear. A very bad strategy for heaven seekers.

Chapter Six
The Truth About Me and How I Would Have Done It

Some Thoughts on Me

Okay, enough about what you guys have made up about Me. I am nothing like you think, and you all think different and incompatible things anyway. I am not pure love, pure energy, pure thought, an unembodied mind, nature, music, a force field, or the Energizer Bunny. I am not omnipresent, All-Powerful, All-Knowing, All-Good, or All-Loving. I am not outside space and time! Stop saying that! As far as I know, I am not necessary to your existence. I may well not be eternal, who knows?

How could love, or pure energy, or nature, think or know things anyway, much less be All-Powerful and All-Loving? Do you know how crazy that sounds? You should definitely consider taking a neurobiology course, or maybe just head directly for a psychiatrist appointment. You can get in line behind the unembodied-mind people. How can an immaterial, unembodied "mind" existing in a place with no matter cause anything material to happen? Did he, she, or they think or will quarks and electrons into existence? That is not how I did it, not even close.

You need to get rid of your pre-existing beliefs. I mean clean the slate. Then think bigger, much bigger. Human-like animals have only been around for a couple hundred thousand years. The dinosaurs lived on earth about eight hundred times longer than that. You are at the blastocyst stage of knowledge. You have just begun to understand a few things about the cosmos. You do not have enough knowledge to figure out what I am or where I came from. You cannot even fuse hydrogen efficiently, for My sake! Maybe someday a million years down the road. Why don't you just admit that, love each other, have fun with your families, and find out after you die? Maybe I will make a visit, or inspire another book, and tell you My Big Secret. It is a pretty cool story, I assure you.

One tip for young people who are looking for answers to the Big Questions anyway—beware of confirmation bias. It exists in everyone, especially among philosophers and religious apologists. This is the tendency of people to favor information that confirms or strengthens their beliefs or values. When a speaker quotes a so-called expert, listen politely to what they have to say. The information may be interesting and persuasive to you, but, in reality, it may represent a minority and a not-very-well-substantiated view. You are unlikely to be told by most apologists that a substantial majority of physicists and cosmologists are non-believers and their reasons why, so don't be fooled by quotes from "experts." Do your own research.

In their grade school catechism, the Catholic Church teaches very young children (first and second graders) that "God is a spirit infinitely perfect," "God had no beginning; He always was and He always will be," and "Man is a creature composed of body and soul and made to the image and likeness of God."[75]

What? Look in a mirror once in a while. Do you imagine you are made in an eternal God's image? You don't look (or think) anything like me! Do you think I waited 13.8 billion years for a creature to evolve in My image, physical or otherwise? How about your genetic forebears that gradually evolved over hundreds of thousands of years to produce your current physical and psychological characteristics? When did they become human, get a soul, and assume My image and likeness? I am going with January 1925, when Paul Newman was born.

Do you all think I have never considered My own role in your universe, and other universes? Do you think I never wonder where I came from, what I am made of, how I can do the things I do, what is My purpose, what are My moral values, where I will go if I cease to exist someday, and especially whether I am an unembodied mind outside of space and time? I think about these things, too.

Don't forget, I am smarter than you and have had a lot of time on My hands. I have spent a couple billion years pondering these questions, and I cannot figure them out! So, where did I come from? What is My purpose? Don't tell Me it is just to reward humans who believe in Me. How boring and inconsequential would that be! I have to exist forever so a couple of you humans can be forgiven for bad behaviors and get to heaven, even though (Spoiler Alert!) your species will soon enough be gone from the face of the planet? Hello!!! Anyone who believes that, please raise your hand. You are going to the back of the heaven line! My purpose must be "infinitely" greater than that. If you have any good ideas, please send Me a text (the pope has My number). Remember, you can also email Me at godinheaven@fabrication.com.

Why can't I have a Creator, too? This question especially drives Me crazy—where did I come from? Did a past deity create Me or am I the First Cause, The Unmoved Mover, The Unstopped Stopper, The Big Banger? Maybe I am that dark matter or energy everyone is looking for. Have I always been here? (My memory fades after about forty billion years ago.)

I have always thought there must be an infinite, All-Good, All-Knowing, All-Powerful, All-Loving Being or Spirit who is everywhere and who created Me, and that eventually I will meet him, her, or them, especially if I do a good job. Maybe he, she, or they are a spirit, or a force, or pure energy, or love, or just nature itself. Does that mean I have a soul? Hey, if you have one, I can have one. Mine has no marks, so, do I go right to heaven where My reward is, and where I don't have to care for you all the time? Even though I am omniscient, All-Good, All-Loving, All-Powerful, and able to leap tall buildings in a single bound, these problems bother and distract Me.

More recently, I am thinking I am in a computer simulation, but I need some more evidence. Let's start with what I know:

First of all, I am not immaterial. How could an immaterial entity create something material from nothing, and then cause that material to do things? That's logically incoherent. (That's Me using philosopher talk!) There are no mirrors at My place, so I have a little trouble telling you what I look like. Just kidding! My basic image is All-Attractive, but I can change it around quite a bit. Sometimes I am a pervasive force of pure energy; sometimes a giant six-limbed anteater, sometimes I am three-Gods-in-one, a Father, Son, and a Holy Spirit. Just kidding! I bet that caused some heart palpitations in some of you Jews and Muslims! I like the pure energy idea because it is more mysterious, and I can confuse you more with that one.

I seem to get around quite a bit, so either I am really fast, or My spirit covers a lot of space. I can travel much faster than the speed of light—and without time dilation. (Take that Einstein!) So, I have My own physics. That should not surprise you. There are lots of universes with different physics that support all kinds of life which you would find fascinating, if it did not eat you first.

I am not everywhere at once. How could I be? Just your own universe is huge! But I have great vision and can easily scan your little rock, so I am pretty up-to-date on what you guys are doing.

As far as I know, it is just Me and a lot of stars, rocks, space dust, and dark matter or energy out here, although I can't be sure. I am much more complicated than you—but, apparently, My Creator only needed to make one of Me (sorry, Hindus), and I have lasted a long time. Why would My Creator just make one of Me? It is pretty lonely and boring for someone with My intelligence to exist alone. I could have used some Godly companionship just for someone to talk to and crack some religion jokes with occasionally. I do like to read. I always wondered what took Guggenheim so long, but anyway, he delivered. And I must tell you those e-readers were a game changer! They came along just in time.

For a while, I felt like I had the spark of an unknown Creator in Me, and I tried meditation to find this spark before I caught fire. In the end, I had the occasional personal experience of a higher being, but soon I realized that this was just something My "mind" was making up, because I wanted so badly to have a Creator who took care of Me. Anyway, I am still hoping I go to some sort of heaven (or at least Florida) when My Creator is done with Me.

I am a very complex guy—so complex, I often think someone or something else (maybe an energy, force, or pure love) created Me in their image because they love Me. This entity must be even more powerful, omniscient, All-Loving, and better-looking than Me. I tend to think he is not the personal contact type, since he has never made himself known to Me. I call him Unknowable. Like you, it makes Me look silly to say he takes care of Me, since there is no evidence for that. It sounds like I am just making that up.

Anyway, I am sure I exist.

Thoughts on My Existence

One line of reasoning for My existence that I like came from you guys. It goes like this:

- God is something than which nothing greater can be thought.

- I can imagine that He exists and is as perfect as possible.

- Existing would be more perfect than not existing.

- Therefore, He exists!

What—you don't find that convincing?? I am going over to talk with Anselm in a few minutes. He told Me this worked extremely well for him back in the eleventh century. Anselm was a monk, abbot, philosopher, and theologian of the Catholic Church, who held the office of Archbishop of Canterbury from 1093 to 1109. After his death, he was canonized as a saint. If you are a fan of Anselm and his ontological argument, I encourage you to read his book *Cur Deus Homo* (Why God Became a Man). Often described as his masterwork, this book is possibly the most contrived and ridiculous book ever written on why it took the incarnation and suffering of the Son of Me to save mankind after Adam and Eve ate a forbidden apple offered by a satanic snake. Okay, I understand it was the eleventh century, and the reason for an incarnation was and is truly baffling, but let's not make stuff up. As Anselm said, "If it be necessary, therefore, as it appears, that the heavenly kingdom be made up of men, and this cannot be effected unless the aforesaid satisfaction [Sacrificing the Son of Me for man's original sin] be made, which none but God can make and none but man ought to make, it is necessary for the God-man to make it."[76]

According to Richard Dawkins, this ontological argument deserves a special mention for being one of the worst arguments in history. He finds it demeaning that some individuals think you can figure out something as grand and important as the universe "by sitting in your armchair and logic-chopping."[77]

In the same publication, when asked how he would respond to the ontological argument, Daniel Dennett says he would stifle a yawn and say, "Give me a break!" He further notes that the description of God as omnipotent, omniscient, and All-Loving is contradictory and hopeless. He finds ontological arguments not that interesting.[78] Hey, I found a philosopher of religion who makes sense! I can imagine that a God exists, too, but, looking around, I can think of a very different God than the one Anselm and you guys pray to, glorify, and worship.

According to Daniel J. Hill, one famous definition of God among philosophers of religion is "the greatest possible being," not just greater than every other being that *actually* exists, but greater than every other being that *could* have existed.[79]

In the same publication, Swinburne describes what he feels the Christian tradition has always meant by God. To Swinburne, God is a perfectly free, personal being who created the universe and who can do anything that is logically possible to do. He knows everything that is logically possible to know, and He always does the best action when there is a best action to do. If there is no best option, God will perform a good action, but never a bad action. That's what Swinburne means when he refers to God.[80]

And that's what I mean by crazy! Why do I have to be perfect? I am not perfect, and I do not know everything. I am a pretty nice person, but I am not All-Good and All-Loving. Sure, I am more powerful than you. I created your universe and let it evolve. That does not mean I am All-Powerful! You just say that I am perfect with absolutely no evidence because you defined Me that way and want it to be true. And stop saying I am unembodied. It is quite possible a physical being created this mess. I could have My own Creator. How would you even know?

And who says existing is more perfect than not existing? Why is that true? Why is existing considered a perfection?

Another classical argument for God's existence is al-Ghazali's version of the cosmological argument. To summarize:

- Everything that begins to exist has a cause.

- The universe began to exist, and therefore the universe has a cause.

- The explanation of the universe's existence must be God.

Well, could you not postulate that the universe has existed forever? If an eternal God doesn't need a cause, neither does an eternal universe. Furthermore, if an eternal universe can exist without a cause, why couldn't a bounded universe that starts in a Big Bang do the same?[81]

In the twelfth century, another "great" religious thinker, St. Thomas Aquinas, invoked Anselm's argument for the self-evidence of God. Thomas' writings included the five arguments for My existence: change, efficient causality, the ground of necessity, the degree of being, and final causes. If you are interested, please read these entertaining arguments. I learned that God is unmoving. If he could move, a prior mover must have moved him. Thomas also notes, "God awakens and causes the motion of things. Therefore, he is love and the creator of love in others."[82]

So, per St. Thomas Aquinas, God woke up, moved some things, and is, therefore, love. Who am I to argue with a great philosopher and theologian? Thomas also noted, "The arrangement of diverse things cannot be dictated by their own private and divergent natures; of themselves they are diverse and have no tendency to make a pattern. It follows that the order of many among themselves is either a matter of chance or it must be resolved into one first planner who has a purpose in mind. What comes about always or in the great majority of cases, is not the result of accident. Therefore, the whole of this world has but one planner or governor."[83] Huh?—I am a Project Manager? No way, those guys bore Me to tears.

Okay—let's forget those old guys who just sat around thinking and making stuff up. How about belief in the existence of God amongst most leading scientists of today?

Membership in the National Academy of Sciences (NAS) is awarded to scientists who have made distinguished and continuing achievements in original research. Members are considered the best of the best scientists. Edward J. Larson and Larry Witham published an article in *Nature*, a leading scientific journal, noting that disbelief in God and disbelief in immortality among NAS biological scientists was 65.2% and 69%, respectively, while among NAS physical scientists it was 79% and 76.3%. Biological scientists had the lowest rate of belief in God (5.5%). Physicists and astronomers (those who actually ponder the universe for a living) were slightly higher at 7.5% belief in God. NAS mathematicians had the highest rate of belief in God at 14.3%. Non-belief has remained fairly consistent among leading scientists since the early twentieth century.[84] The use of these polls is not a *post hoc propter hoc* fallacy. You can argue methodologic differences, but the bottom line is obvious: leading scientists, including those who do cosmology for a living, are very unlikely to believe in God or immortality.

Are there modern-day thinkers, a renowned scientist perhaps, who believe in a Supreme Being? Well, Dr. Francis S. Collins would seem to fit the bill. Dr. Collins led the Human Genome Project and was named to lead the National Institutes of Health. He is a very bright guy who has contributed significantly to the scientific progress of mankind. He has also written a book entitled *The Language of God: A Scientist Presents Evidence for Belief.*

The human genome consists of some three billion "letters" and contains the hereditary code of life which directs one initial cell to develop into a living human being. The adult human body contains roughly thirty trillion cells—that is some instruction book![85] When a male sperm and female egg combine, this "instruction book" is passed from parents to children. Upon publication of the human genome sequence, Dr. Collins noted that it is was humbling and awe-inspiring to have caught the first glimpse of our own instruction book, previously known only to God.[86]

Actually, the published code was quite a surprise even for Me! I noticed right away that I misplaced several pretty important letters. And who would have guessed mutations and other errors occur when the three billion letters of DNA get copied over and over? The night of the announcement, I could not sleep at all! I had wondered where all those birth defects and hereditary diseases came from, not to mention your tendencies toward diabetes, heart disease, and cancer. Maybe I will fix some of these coding errors, or perhaps I will just let it go—you have to die from something, or you will never get to heaven!

Dr. Collins felt the elucidation of the code was an occasion for worship. Hey—stop worshiping Me! Why are you doing that? Would an All-Good and All-Loving God want his creatures to worship him? Maybe an All-Arrogant one. I do not want people worshiping Me. Go out and help someone and stop wasting your time. I guess Dr. Collins just has to worship and pray to the Big Geneticist in the sky.

Dr. Collins believes in a personal God who is unlimited by time and space and takes a personal interest in each one of you. He leads one to believe that he was not especially religious while growing up. However, when he was just five years old, his parents sent him and a brother to become members of an Episcopalian Church choir. Like most people, he remembers what his parents told him at five years of age. He remembers being told that joining the choir was to learn music and not to take the theology too seriously. Like most five-year-olds, he was unaffected by the preaching in the church. (Anybody's B.S. meter sounding an alarm?)

In his early teens, Dr. Collins had the experience of longing for something outside himself often associated with the beauty of nature. He notes his feelings were easily challenged by the one or two "aggressive atheists" found in every college dorm. Let's face it, Dr. Collins really wants to believe in a benevolent Supreme Being watching over all of us (and especially him), but he cannot carry the argument. He becomes an agnostic and then an atheist.

After entering medical school, Dr. Collins had a spiritual crisis following a discussion with an ailing patient who was surprised when Dr. Collins admitted he was not sure what he believed. He consulted a Methodist minister (who else would an atheist consult?) who suggested he read *Mere Christianity* by C.S. Lewis. Dr. Collins did and was especially impacted by Lewis' comments on the existence of the moral law or "the law of right behavior." Apparently, the fact that the concept of right and wrong exists among almost all humans makes the concept approach the status of a law, like the law of gravitation or special relativity. (Tip from God—No it doesn't!)

Lewis commented that, if there was a controlling power outside the universe (like Me, for example), it could reveal itself to people inside the universe no more than the architect of a house could be a wall or staircase or fireplace in that house. The only way this power could show itself would be inside ourselves as an influence (like the moral law) trying to get us to act in a certain way. Surely, Lewis felt, this ought to arouse our suspicions?[87] Well, surely you should meet your architect before any building begins. If he turns out to be a staircase or a fireplace, hire someone else. Also, I am a bit confused on how a power outside the universe cannot show itself inside our universe, but can influence us inside the universe—how does that work, exactly?

As an aside, perhaps a few more musings from C.S. Lewis whom some have called the greatest Christian thinker of the twentieth century. The following summarizes Lewis' thoughts on the topic of marriage:

Lewis notes that Christian wives promise to obey their husbands, who are said to be the head of the household. Apparently, in order to have a successful marriage either the husband or wife must be the decider of family policy. You cannot have a lasting marriage "without a constitution." So, why should the man be the head? Lewis questions whether anyone seriously wishes for the woman to be the head of the family. He feels it is unnatural for the wife to rule over the husband. According to Lewis, this is because the mother's chief purpose in life is to protect her children and husband. This naturally clouds her judgment. The husband will be much more just to outsiders. He can protect others from the intense familial prejudices of the wife.[88]

Having now seen how Mr. Lewis can make such a well-thought-out and reasoned argument for how a marriage should work, I am sure you understand how he got such a reputation for building arguments in other areas, such as Christianity. I encourage you to read *Mere Christianity*, but don't laugh too hard—you might wake the children.

Dr. Collins writes that when he encountered Lewis' moral law argument when he was twenty-six years of age, he was stunned by its logic. Dr. Collins decides the existence of the moral law can be described as God looking back at him, a God who desires a special relationship with human beings. He has instilled into each one of us a special glimpse of Himself.[89]

On the topic of the Bible, Dr. Collins asks whether it would have served God's purposes thirty-four hundred years ago to lecture to His people about radioactive decay, geologic strata, and DNA?[90]

Well, the answer to that question is "Yes," of course. First of all, Dr. Collins has no idea what My intentions were when the spirit part of Me inspired those Bible books. It was certainly not to "reveal the nature of God to humankind." If that was the case, the first book of the Bible would have been titled "The Nature of God as Revealed to Humankind."

Dr. Collins talks about My purposes thirty-four hundred years ago but skips the fact that the New Testament with My-inspired Gospels, Paul's letters, etc., were written and selected as "inspired" less than two thousand years ago. The timing does not really matter, as the Bible books were presumably written for all humans for all time. So, a little genetic code info or even just a flying buttress description would have helped you guys along quite a bit. Maybe a hint that the Earth is round and circles the Sun would have been good, or that there were ten billion trillion more suns and lots of other planets out there, a warning to not build on a fault line, or perhaps an infectious disease chapter including a section how to make antibiotics and vaccines, or just the importance of cooking your food thoroughly, washing your hands when delivering a baby, mosquito nets, how to handle sewage, better irrigation methods, crop rotation, and other agricultural methods, etc. . . . Even some hints about the existence of atoms, fossil fuels (right below your feet, for My sake!), evolution, electronics, quantum theory, how to win at poker, and maybe a stock tip or two! (Personally, I made a fortune on Amazon.) Statements encouraging seatbelts, or stating you shouldn't give flying lessons to people who don't want to learn how to land, or saying don't buy Betamax, would have caused some confusion back then, but eventually, it would have been pretty useful information. Avoid fascists at all times would have been useful, too. Now that I think about it, how about "No Crucifixions"?? That would have helped out the Son of Me quite a bit!

Dr. Collins goes on to discuss Genesis, atheism, agnosticism, creationism, and intelligent design, among other topics. In My Godly opinion, there is an awful lot of abstract reasoning based on faulty (or absent) evidence and some pretty crazy conclusions drawn on this "evidence." He relates that before he became a believer, the idea that God could become man and suffer death on our behalf (doing it "perfectly" because he was God—remind you of anyone?) sounded like utter nonsense.[91] Guess what, Dr. Collins—you were right!

In the end, the teachings of the male chauvinist, C.S. Lewis, especially the existence of the moral law within us, and the majesty and beauty of God's worldly creation, convinced Dr. Collins there was a God. Finally, Dr. Collins describes a hike he took in the Cascade Mountains while on his first trip west of the Mississippi. He expresses how the majesty and beauty of God's creation overwhelmed his resistance. When he hiked around a corner, he was surprised and startled by a beautiful frozen waterfall, hundreds of feet high. The next morning while the sun was rising, Dr. Collins knelt in the grass and surrendered to Jesus Christ.[92]

Not only do I exist, but I am All-Good. Here is well-known, modern-day, leading Christian apologist and Molinist, William Lane Craig, on Anselm and the God is All-Good issue:

"God is a being worthy of worship. Any being that is not worthy of worship is not God. And, therefore, God must be perfectly good and essentially good. More than that, as Anselm saw, God is the greatest conceivable being, and therefore he is the very paradigm of goodness itself. He is the greatest good. So, once you understand the concept of God, you can see that asking, 'Well, why is God good?' is sort of like asking, 'Why are all bachelors unmarried?' It's the very concept of the greatest conceivable being, of being worthy of worship, that entails the essential goodness of God."[93]

Holy Molinist! Craig, and others of his ilk, define God the way they want and need Me to be and then say it must be an accurate description. Well, you should stop making stuff up about Me with no evidence. It makes you look foolish. And why are all bachelors unmarried anyway?

What, still not convinced that I am not perfect? How about this from Craig on the problem of an All-Powerful, All-Knowing, and All-Loving God allowing humans to choose to do bad things? He claims God has middle knowledge:

"And the Molinist view is that God has this sort of knowledge logically prior to his divine creative decree of a world. . . . What Molinism holds is that since human beings have genuine moral freedom to make choices, God knowing how they would choose in various circumstances allows them to make sinful decisions that he does not directly will. By God's absolute will, he wills everything good. In every moral situation, God wills that a person do the right thing. But he knows that in many cases people would not do the right thing. They would choose to do evil. And so he permits them to do that evil with a view toward achieving his ultimate purposes. So, God's ultimate plan and providential purpose is achieved not by overriding human free will but precisely through the free and sometimes sinful actions of human beings."[94]

Now I get it!

Well, how about natural evil (non-moral evil) like hurricanes, earthquakes, tornadoes, floods, disease, etc.? Craig believes these non-moral evils are within God's right to impose on us and are inflicted on us for a greater good that God wants to achieve and whose rationale we are not expected to understand, given our limited knowledge of God's overall plan.[95]

Here we go again—natural evil is good for you in the long run! I work in mysterious ways, so you do not know what that ultimate good will be. Just have some faith and trust Me on this. So, yes, true believers will tie themselves up in philosophical knots to maintain a Supreme Being who is All-Good, All-Loving, All-Powerful, All-Knowing, and is everywhere forever. When scientists are confronted with new evidence, they change their thinking to accommodate the evidence. When religious people are confronted with new evidence, they will make up whatever bizarre arguments they can to *not* change their beliefs.

As a Christian apologist, what Craig should really apologize for is publishing *What is God Like*, a set of children's books for kids as young as four to eight years old, which covers the attributes of God including God is All-Good, God is All-Powerful, God is self-sufficient, God is spirit, and God is three persons. Nothing like getting a head start on the brainwashing!

Okay, move over Saints Anselm, Augustine, and Thomas Aquinas, and C.S. Lewis. It seems there are lots more people willing to say and believe anything to quell their inner turmoil over why people exist and their "purpose" in life. I wish you would all just relax, work hard, be nice to each other, raise nice families, and eventually die. If I exist, and there is an afterlife, you will know all about it. Until then—it's My secret!

Many humans feel that there must be some "reason" they are here, and there is a Supernatural Being out there just for them—that they are not just bodies full of DNA and other chemicals, and that there will be something after this life.

So, what does a person say to convince you of something he wants to believe so much, that he has convinced himself of it with absolutely no factual evidence? I encourage you to read Saints Anselm, Thomas Aquinas, and Augustine, as well as C.S. Lewis and Dr. Collins to find out. If you like tying yourself up in philosophical knots to keep everything the way it was when you were younger and during your subsequent religious schooling, William Lane Craig would be good for you, too.

Apparently, even otherwise very intelligent humans, who can function well (or even exceedingly well) in their chosen careers and/or family lives, can compartmentalize their faith, feelings, and beliefs in a part of the brain called the "Religion—Don't Touch" lobe, which, of course, contains the "Meaning and Purpose of Life" gyrus. I am not sure how, but there is no doubt that you do this.

When discussing whether God exists or whether he, she, or they are perfect, or if space and time existed before the Big Bang, or how life sprang from inanimate chemicals, or what is consciousness, etc., etc., why are you so afraid of saying, "I don't know."? Try it, it feels really good to admit the truth.

Has it not occurred to philosophers of religion that maybe it is a little early in mankind's development to answer these questions? Again, I am sorry you were born so recently. *Homo sapiens* have existed as a species for maybe five hundred thousand years. The dinosaurs were on Earth for 165 million years! Let's see what earthlings know about the cosmos and neuroscience in just ten thousand more years. They will be justifiably amused at your current level of progress in science and the beliefs of your religious apologists. Having said this, go ahead and speculate all you want. It is kind of fun. Just admit you are speculating (sometimes wildly) based on dramatically insufficient evidence.

"Men willingly believe what they wish." - Julius Caesar, *De Bello Gallico* (100 BCE - 44 BCE)[96]

"A man is his own easiest dupe, for what he wishes to be true he generally believes to be true." - Demosthenes, Greek Statesman (382 BCE - 322 BCE)[97]

But, before you decide this book is making you too uncomfortable, or it is just wrong (but, I am All-Knowledgeable!), I encourage you to read an insightful book titled *The Righteous Mind—Why Good People Are Divided by Politics and Religion* by Jonathan Haidt. Some say I personally inspired him to write this book, although I will deny it, if asked.

Haidt is a moral psychologist. His book (with substantial supporting data) argues that:

- Intuitions come first, and strategic reasoning in support of that intuition comes second. "If you think that moral reasoning is something we do to figure out the truth, you will be constantly frustrated by how foolish, biased, and illogical people become when they disagree with you. But if you think about moral reasoning as a skill we humans evolved to further our social agendas, to justify our own actions, and to defend the teams we belong to—then things will make a lot more sense. Keep your eye on the intuitions, and don't take people's moral arguments at face value. They're mostly post hoc constructions made up on the fly, crafted to advance one or more strategic objectives."[98]

This explains why a presidential candidate who brags about grabbing women by the private parts, has affairs with a Playboy Bunny and a porn star and pays them hush money, was found guilty in a civil case involving sexual molestation, has an extensive record of lying, lacks tolerance and empathy, attempted to reverse a free and fair election, and threatens violence to his detractors all while siding with Russian and North Korean dictators, can be the darling of the majority of Evangelical Christians. They like him intuitively and will support his candidacy no matter what. Many believe he was sent by God! (No, I didn't!)

- There is more to morality than harm or fairness, such as liberty, loyalty, authority, and sanctity.

- Morality binds and blinds. Human nature was produced by natural selection working at two levels at the same time. Individuals compete with individuals within every group, but groups also compete with each other. Humans under certain circumstances are capable of acting for the greater good of the group, like bees in a hive. This enables altruism and heroism, but also war and genocide.

- Haidt writes, "Religion is (probably) an evolutionary adaptation for binding groups together and helping them to create communities with a shared morality. People bind themselves into political teams that share moral narratives. Once they accept a particular narrative, they become blind to alternative moral worlds."

- "True believers produce pious fantasies that don't match reality, and at some point somebody comes along to knock the idol off its pedestal. That was [David] Hume's project, with his philosophically sacrilegious claim that reason was nothing but the servant of the passions."[99]

So Haidt argues (again supported by study data) that we react intuitively (with "gut feelings") to issues and then construct a moral reasoning argument to support our initial intuitive response. Moral reasoning is mostly just a post hoc search for reasons to justify judgments people have already made.[100]

People have an immediate intuitive response when questions on the existence of a Supreme Being or the suitability of presidential candidates arise. Post hoc arguments are then constructed "supporting" their position. The degree to which these post hoc arguments can be convoluted and lacking in evidence can be impressive indeed (see above).

Of course, I am God, so My intuitions and moral reasoning are perfect and All-Good. So, don't argue with Me, or I'll put you in limbo for an extra decade or two with no television and a guy with foot fungus for a roommate. In the end, I feel like I exist, but maybe I don't. You may find out someday.

How Do I Manage Things?

Firstly, I am more of a delegator than a hands-on manager. I have lots of angels, and even archangels, to help Me out. Each one of you gets a guardian angel when you are born to protect you and help guide your behaviors (unfortunately, some guardian angels are better than others). I have archangels to run messages to various prophets and virgin mothers. As you might surmise, My IT department is quite large and is chiefly responsible for monitoring and reporting on the stars, planets, and life in My universes. Each universe has a very experienced team with an executive VP reporting directly to Me.

I generally start My day sitting on a throne in the morning with a good newspaper. I don't need to eat, but because it tastes so good, I usually sit at my heavenly kitchen table with Peter and scarf down some pancakes, scrambled eggs, and bacon before inspiring a couple of holy books. I then walk around heaven for a bit, always checking the electrified fences between the humans, chickens, and cows before I visit a little with Judas, who mans the main entry gate. You have to watch Judas because, for just thirty pieces of silver, he will let almost anyone in here. I then spend a little time going over messages with Michael and Gabriel before listening to each of your prayers from the previous day. After deciding which football teams will win, the rest of the day is devoted to My main project—Judgment Day. The logistics of this future event are very, very challenging, even for Me.

I am going as fast as I can, because there are a lot of rotting bodies out there, waiting to be reunited with their souls. It is estimated that since anatomically modern humans arose about 190 thousand years ago, about 120 billion humans have lived on Earth.[101] Therefore, since only 8 billion humans are alive today, I have to find and identify 112 billion dead bodies, mostly without faces, and match them with their individual souls, wherever they may be. Of course, I still need to care for those other 120 billion souls from embryos that did not make it. One pretty big problem I have is that souls are invisible. I travel around most nights to purgatory, limbo, heaven, and various gravesites spraying foot powder in the air, attempting to locate all the souls I can, in order to check their serial numbers. Anyway, I'll get it done.

I have already arranged for a great trumpeter to announce that the Big Day is upon you. After the trumpet blast, he will play a few classic jazz pieces to calm you back down. Then there will be a few strange and terrible events (maybe a MAGA rally followed by a U.S. House of Representatives Oversight Committee hearing).

Then comes the judging part of Judgment Day. All humans who have ever lived will be judged by Me based on what you have said and done. Then you get the thumbs-up or thumbs-down. I like to draw that part out a bit. Some of you think I will be sitting on a great white throne. Maybe, but since this is going to take a while, I am thinking of My favorite heavenly Barcalounger. Periodic foot massages by Mary Magdalene may be part of the program, with special emphasis on those nail hole areas.

Then the thumbs-up people have to be moved to heaven, where they will live happily ever after, while the thumbs-down folks have to be moved to hell, where they will live forever in a painful, fiery place. Well, Damnation! Eighty years on Earth and infinity in hell. I guess I am not All-Fair.

A few of you who did some pretty bad things, but otherwise led a good life, will have those bad things burned off in purgatory and then advance to heaven. Believe Me, it will hurt a bit, but it is certainly worth it. SPF 100 is highly recommended.

So, unfortunately, Judgment Day is still a ways off. Hopefully, I will get it done before your Sun engulfs you in a few billion years. Maybe you will figure out how to safely travel to another planet or solar system and establish your human race there. Wouldn't it be funny if I got Judgment Day all arranged, blew "Reveille" on the trumpet, and descended upon Earth, only to discover you had moved somewhere else! That would really irritate Me!

Am I Everywhere? Do I work at a distance? Do I warp space-time? Hey, I sound like gravity. Gravity is definitely a universal force. Am I composed of gravitons? I am going to leave that one unanswered until Judgment Day.

How do I keep tabs on everything happening in My universe(s)? Well, I can't, obviously. That's what all those angels and IT people are for. I am constantly looking to minimize all these galaxy collisions, quasars, novas and supernovas, black hole events, etc. Certainly, it is tough to catch every little meteorite, earthquake, tsunami, volcano, cosmic ray burst, etc. Just ask the dinosaurs and those green squiggly things that used to live on Mars.

Let's finish the Bible discussion. Generally, I am an honest God and very transparent. If I were inspiring books to guide humanity I would have very clearly and directly told you everything about Me, your place in the universe, and provided explicit guidelines for the behaviors I expected. Why all the mystery???

Of course, I would have provided you with all sorts of information on how to make your lives easier from scientific, engineering, and societal perspectives. And why haven't I inspired more books along the way? Why did I stop inspiring Hindus over three thousand years ago, most Christians two thousand years ago, and Muslims thirteen hundred years ago? That makes no sense.

I could help you with lots of things. For example, you guys are having a fair amount of trouble coming up with a useful and economically feasible fusion reactor design. These reactors will use nuclear fusion, the process that powers the Sun and other stars, to produce electric power without carbon emissions, long-lived nuclear waste, or risk of meltdowns.[102] You are probably a few decades or more (Hint: think a lot more) away from success in this area. When you figure it out, it will be transformative for your planet. Well, the answers are actually pretty simple. I am thinking of becoming a burning plasma and speaking to one of your physicist prophets about this so he can write it down in an inspired book. Let's call it The Book of Einstein. We can add it to the New Testament right after The Book of Revelation. Everyone can go out to a fusion restaurant to celebrate.

By the way, I came up with some edits for the first couple of Testaments. Word of mouth is not that accurate, and your transcribers made quite a few mistakes along the way. First of all, I said, "The Geek will inherit the Earth," not the Meek. I was thinking of Bill Gates at the time, and I was right again!

And, as you all know, a star could not have been over the stable in Bethlehem. Long before the straw in that place would have gone up in flames, the gravity effects would have ripped your planet and everything on it into a million pieces. There is no way I could have stopped that! That star was just some Christmas lights I used to guide those three wise men.

Of course, I have to add something on dark energy and dark matter to Genesis. There are lots of other physics and chemistry ideas I need to mention, along with info on a few thousand new species, some important medical findings, a ban on fascism, and there are a couple good books I want to recommend. Also, I want to say that the LGBTQ+ community is okay in my book—hey, why not? Being true to yourselves is very important.

One great part of your Bible covers My Sermon on the Mount—one of My finer efforts. It was too long to memorize, so I had to use a teleprompter on that one! Still, My delivery was excellent. And those loaves and fishes kept all the little kids quiet for almost the whole thing. (We had to send out five or six times for all that food.) Pay attention, there are some good things in there!

Now, let's be serious. If I wanted a Bible or other holy book, I would have written it Myself. Why would I let you guys pick some books for the Bible? Raise your hand if you think God is too lazy to write Bible books, so he inspired others to do it and then let humans pick the books they liked best. Ah—I see you have learned not to raise your hands so fast. You are correct!

Those who believe I inspired humans to write Bible books will have a special place in the heavenly library where they will be forced to only read bad fiction with an emphasis on science fiction and fantasy. You can read the Bible, Qur'an, Bhagavad Gita, Torah, and Book of Mormon all day long. If you get bored,

I have thrown in a few books by Clarke, Asimov, and Heinlein along with some *Star Trek* DVDs.

There was absolutely no need for you guys to author My Bible, the Qur'an, or the Vedas. I would have told all of you everything you need to know in a direct and transparent manner, something everyone in the world could see, read, hear about, and understand. If I wanted to save all you guys, I would have appeared before everyone at the same time (I'm God, I can do that) and clarified the situation and what you had to do moving forward.

The Son of Me argued with Me about his incarnation, but I wanted him to be born to the virgin wife of a backwater carpenter and live in the middle of nowhere for thirty years, then wander the countryside with twelve of his buddies for the next three years, before trashing a temple, getting arrested, implying he was King of the Jews, getting sentenced to death, and hanging on a cross for three hours. I was convinced that was the best way to get you back on the straight and narrow. He argued that it was My idea, so maybe I should be the one to have nails hammered through his hands and feet. Unfortunately for him, he couldn't convince Me.

NOW PAY ATTENTION!

YOUR LIFE IS NOT A TEST TO SEE WHO LOVES ME THE MOST OR BELIEVES IN MY RESURRECTION AND ASCENSION.

STOP FIGHTING OVER WHETHER I AM ONE GOD OR A THREE-IN-ONE GOD OR MANY GODS.

JUST FOLLOW MY GUIDELINES AND GET ALONG WITH EACH OTHER.

HAVE A LITTLE FUN.

There is no Supernatural Being watching over everything you do and reading your thoughts (just you, Father Riley!).

My guidelines are easy—I got most of them from My atheist and agnostic friends!

Treat your neighbor as you would have them treat you.

Stop fighting with each other. Respect everyone's right to their own opinion, if it is an informed opinion. No wars! What is wrong with you people? I have landmined a fairly large section of the firmament in heaven where all those responsible for initiating a major conflict will live. See how you like it!

I would never allow a professional clergy. That means no priests, pastors, reverends, mullahs, imams, rabbis, pujaris, monks, or anyone else wearing funny clothes and proclaiming they know all about Me while asking for your money. There would certainly be no lifetime professional politicians. There would be term limits—and short terms at that!

Try to imagine how things would be if there was a truly All-Good, All-Powerful, All-Loving, All-Knowing God versus Something Else:

All-Everything God	Something Else
Very strong evidence for God	No strong evidence
God is knowable	God is unknowable
No Mystery	Lots of Mystery
God communicates regularly with everyone	No communication with everyone
Bible would be a clear set of rules/ guidelines full of useful information	Poorly written and confusing text that requires interpretation, lacking in useful information
Holy books directly from God	Books "inspired" and chosen by humans
One universal set of religious doctrines	Doctrines differ by religion
Universe and creatures created simultaneously	Fourteen billion years and extinctions/evolution

No problem of evil	Moral evil and natural disasters exist
No wars	Lots of wars
No suffering	Lots of suffering
Equality of wealth/circumstances	Lots of inequality of wealth/circumstances
Life enjoyable without struggle for all creatures	Constant struggle for survival
Women treated equally	Patriarchal societies
No worship	Worship required
No House Oversight Committee	House Oversight Committee exists

Hmmm, it looks like "Something Else" is the honest conclusion down there.

If I was omniscient, All-Powerful, All-Good, and All-Loving, here is How I Would Have Done It:

Since I need company, I would create roughly 10^{11} galaxies with about 10^{11} stars in each one. There would be roughly 10^{22} planets in your universe (10,000,000,000,000,000,000,000 planets). If I allowed life on one in a billion of these planets, that would be ten trillion planets capable of supporting life in the universe. So, you would not be My main squeeze, if you catch My drift. However, I would take great care of all My life, including My earthly humans.

My Holy Book would have been written by Me for everyone for all ages! Why would I inspire a bunch of confusing writings whose authorship is often unknown, and which in the Christian tradition were designated as sacred scripture 350 years after Christ lived by a bunch of ignorant bishops and church officials, and subsequently presented to varying small populations of superstitious people?

I would have told you many facts about your universe, describing atoms, chemistry, physics, biology, medicine, architecture, art, music, and literature. My Holy Book would have explicitly described Me and how I created your universe and everything in it. I would have detailed My plans for everything, living or not living. There are no mysteries here—why make everything mysterious? I do not "work in mysterious ways." Why would I?

I would personally hand-deliver a set of guidelines for everyone entitled "How to Lead a Good Life." Follow these guidelines, and I will consider something nice for you, something between a gift certificate to Starbucks and everlasting life. Ignore these guidelines, and I will disappear you when you die (maybe before). Or maybe I will force you to join a couples' book club for a year and then give you one more chance.

Lucky for you there is no hell. Only a mean jerk God would put you in hell. (Although on a particularly bad day, I have considered turning up the heat in the room for a couple of you lawyers and politicians.)

There is no getting into heaven just because you believe in Me and that the Son of Me rose from the dead! Others say you will have a better chance if you refrain from doing evil, do good works, are truthful, kind, and feed the needy. You are getting warmer! Also, some say if you blow up a nice building full of people who oppose your beliefs, you can get in the express lane to heaven. Nice try, but you will have to do better than that!

By the way, maybe you can tell I am not the All-Loving God some of your religious leaders profess Me to be. How would they know? Man, I really dislike those know-it-alls. I have My ups and downs like anyone else, but, in general, I am a pretty good guy. Trust Me on this one (you sort of have to).

Actually, since I love all of you, I would have made all My creatures' lives perfect from the get-go. I would make frequent trips to your planet on a pre-announced schedule, so everyone could hear what I have to say. Your lives would certainly not be a test to see who gets rewarded for eternity. Imagine having a Supreme Proctor for your God! What kind of All-Knowing and All-Loving God would create someone, knowing ahead of time that they are going to make a mistake and burn forever? Who thinks I am that evil? Oh, I forgot about that Middle Knowledge fabrication.

Anyway, nobody is allowed to misbehave, and everyone gets into paradise (eventually).

There would be no evil in the universe and no suffering on your planet. What good would that do? My Holy Book would leave a few gaps in the details for you to discover on your own. That's part of the fun of it. Otherwise, why would I have you spend eighty years or so working away on that tiny rock before you get to heaven? I don't want you to get bored!

Maybe I will change things so you go straight to heaven when you are created. That makes more sense to Me. The creatures I love can be with Me all the time and not have to go through a trial period down on Earth. That saves Me a lot of time on Judgment Day, and the three million kids who would have starved to death each year get a Happy Meal for lunch every day (with two toys inside)!

As for work—there would be no actual "jobs." You can work if you want, but it is not necessary. Just have a good time—it's on Me! Why would I make ninety percent of you do something you did not really want to do for eight to ten hours a day, before sleeping another eight to ten hours? Why would I create marketing people or personal injury lawyers, for My sakes? Everyone would be comfortable and treated the same. There would be an equal distribution of goods.

Shelter, clothes, and transportation would be free. I would supply food and water to all My living creatures, so you don't have to kill and eat each other. Violence of any kind would be *verboten*. Just spend time with your families and friends, travel a bit, and enjoy life. If studying or inventing things makes you happy, go for it.

It would be important to realize that sucking up to Me can get you disappeared. Anyone praying to Me or worshiping Me should stockpile a few cases of SPF 100+ sunscreen and some zinc oxide.

There would be no Saturday or Sunday services, no worship of Me of any kind, and no requirements for funny-looking hats, haircuts, beards, prayer beads, or rugs. Go to the beach, take a walk, or watch a movie with your kids, for Pete's sake.

I do insist on some new eating parameters, however. Commandment #11: Stop eating all My creatures!!!! Did you know farmed poultry makes up 70% of all birds on the planet and that 60% of all mammals on Earth are livestock, mostly cattle and pigs?[103] No more eating My animals, including My fish. And, hey, why do you think I made all those plants that are just sitting there rooted to the ground??? They are for you! Consider them a gift from God. Eat as much as you can and make sure everyone gets some. I just decided vegetarians are getting in first up here. The rest of you will spend a little time in the Zoo near the cattle, chicken, and fish areas.

There would be no wars, starvation, authoritarian or totalitarian governments, volcanoes, tornados, hurricanes, floods, earth-

quakes, poverty, disease, religions, other tribal entities, conservative talk radio, etc., etc. Nobody would get sick, not even
a runny nose. There would be some good water for Flint,
Michigan, too.

Women and minorities would be treated the same as white
men—make that better than white men. (Makeup call!)

No More Mystery!!

You have believed in Me or something like Me for many
thousands of years with no evidence—how anti-intellectual.
Maybe this has been due to your upbringing, societal pres-
sures, desire for psychological comfort, or your small brains.
In reality, you are being intellectually lazy. Put in the work,
and maybe I will cut back on your limbo time. Some of you
"just feel" there is a purpose or meaning to life and everything
happens for a reason. Well, I "just feel" like sending you to live
in a very hot place. Maybe you have been listening to all those
theologians, philosophers, and religious apologists who have
been making stuff up out of whole cloth over the years.

Please believe this: you cannot reason Me into existence. But
you don't have to worry, because now that you humans have
made a little progress, I will definitely prove My existence by
making annual televised appearances on Earth, probably at half-
time during the Super Bowl, where I will make a good speech,
with simultaneous translations by several archangels, and sing

the Philadelphia Eagles fight song before I return to heaven. Loaves and fishes for everyone!

If I were God, in order to further demonstrate My existence and superpowers, I would perform very public miracles for you from time to time. I am very entertaining! After a few All-Funny jokes, I could start with some sleight-of-hand or really good card tricks, and after I am warmed up, maybe I would fly around a little, or raise someone from the dead, or maybe even stop the Earth from spinning for a few minutes. You would not like that one, I promise, although you might enjoy the first couple minutes of flight time. I tried something similar a couple light years away, and now I have to start all over again there.

Sorry, but I have to tell you, there is no underlying purpose or meaning to life, other than breaking eighty on the golf course. Just love your family, work hard, admire your beautiful universe, and enjoy the fact that some thirty trillion cells defied all the odds, and you are here! Hey—that's a miracle!!!

And by the way, none of you guys have had a "personal experience" with Me. I would know! Just not My style. Why would I share an experience with just one of you at a time? Remember—God does not play favorites! If you have had an "experience," please talk with someone and maybe get some meds.

And let's discuss your other propaganda declaration that without Me there is no moral foundation for your behavior. There would be no meaning to life. Without Me and a promise of an afterlife, you might as well cut your children in half since it does not matter. You wanna say that to My face? You must stop making stuff up—God does not like it! This is pure, unmitigated, made-up B.S., and you know it. I am really going to punish anyone who argues this point of view. If you think you have to believe in Me to come up with moral guidelines, you are either totally brainwashed, or, at your core, you are a very bad person.

Do you need a commandment from Me to tell you to not kill or steal? If you answer yes to this question, I know who you are. I made a big mistake with you, and I am going to mess with most of your fertility genes.

There would be no talking about religion with your children until they are old enough to really understand. Let's say at least eighteen years old.

Evolution would continue to be taught in schools since it is the truth. (Nice job, Darwin!) My Holy Book would have a few surprises in the Book of Evolution which will cover another few billion years. Sorry, but I did not start this whole process fourteen billion years ago with you in mind as the end product on Earth. There are lots of future species coming here and elsewhere in My universe—isn't that obvious? You evolved in just a couple billion years after the Earth formed some four to five billion years ago. There are trillions of other planets and many of them can support some form of life. You guys are kind of cool (I mean you can reproduce, cultivate the land to feed yourselves, design rocket ships, and perform neurosurgery), but each of you only lasts eighty years or so, and you are kind of ugly, so get used to it—better things are coming. After all, 99.9% of all previous species are gone, and pretty soon you will be gone too.

Okay, so how are you guys doing so far? I have to tell you it has been kind of a slow start. Let's go over it again. *Homo sapiens* ("wise humans") appeared roughly five hundred thousand years ago. More anatomically modern *Homo sapiens* evolved about two hundred thousand years ago. It was not until about forty thousand years ago that more complex and innovative cultures appeared and included behavior that would be recognized as typical of modern humans today.[104]

The Neolithic Revolution, also called the Agricultural Revolution, started around 10,000 BCE and marked the transition in human history from small, nomadic bands of hunter-gatherers to larger, agricultural settlements and early civilization.[105]

Your development is so slow, it is like watching a solar system form. However, since you basically just reached the civilization stage, I am going to give you some more time—but let's pick up the pace a little.

Those Dark Ages and Middle Ages were so depressing, that I have to admit I seriously considered moving up the date of Judgment Day. You guys liked to fight and came up with some pretty innovative weapons to maim and kill each other, from swords and spears to maces, axes, crossbows, and longbows. The trebuchet was kind of cool, but your invention of gunpowder was a real innovation in the human killing arena. Torture was all the rage for a time, especially with the rack, thumbscrews, knee-splitters, and breaking wheels as key tools of the Inquisitions.

I am telling you, the Son of Me was pretty pissed off that all this happened after he sacrificed his human life for you and ended up with pretty severe ankle and wrist arthritis for the effort.

The Renaissance encouraged Me a bit (just when I was thinking of an extinction event for you), but more recently you are looking bad again with the hate index achieving record levels, and regional and global wars becoming all the rage. Ultimately, you have invented nuclear weapons, and now you can eradicate yourselves without My help. Don't worry, I won't let that happen, not after all My Judgment Day planning.

Donald Trump? C'mon, you can do better! When Trump was elected, it made Me mad, but I went with it. I am warning you to never, ever say I chose a total gaslighter to head up the most powerful country on Earth. Anyone who does that will join him at the big, never-ending marshmallow roast.

Is this the world you think an Almighty God would have come up with? Well, if you answered "Yes," I gotta tell you, I am pretty insulted.

Let's Be Honest

This is going to be somewhat repetitive and the toughest section for many of you. I am going to repeat some facts for you, and you are going to admit how short a time humans have existed on your planet, and how little you know about the cosmos and the origins of your universe and life.

That is okay. It's early.

Let's cover a few milestones.

Milestone	Date
Anatomically modern *Homo sapiens* appears	200,000 BCE
Farming and first communities	10,000 BCE
Printing press	~1440 CE
Telescopes	1608 CE
Newton's laws of motion and gravity	1686 CE
Edison light bulb	1879 CE
Automobiles	1886 CE
Wright brothers' powered flights	1903 CE

Einstein's special relativity	1905 CE
Einstein's general relativity	1915 CE
Galaxies exist beyond Milky Way and quantum mechanics	1925 CE
Big Bang Theory of universe	1931 CE
Man on Moon	1969 CE
Personal computers	~1977 CE
Cell phones publicly available	~1983 CE
Hubble Space Telescope	1990 CE
James Webb Space Telescope	2021 CE

The dinosaurs, many of whom were predators and spent all day hunting and killing each other for food, were smarter than you think, but not as smart as you humans. They lasted 165 million years, and it took a big meteor to take them out.

So, at twelve thousand years since farming began, and fifty years since personal computers, it would be fair to say that in the absence of large meteor impacts, major nuclear wars, lethal climate change, or a totally new microbe that kills everyone, you probably have millions of years remaining on this planet—perhaps hundreds of millions. I am sorry you are at the zygote phase of humanity. In just the next few thousand years, there will be many, many exciting and awe-inspiring discoveries coming in the fields of physics, cosmology, chemistry, material science, computer science, engineering, artificial intelligence, medicine, novel energy sources, space travel, neuroscience, and other biological fields, etc., etc. There will be no discoveries by today's traditional organized religions, unless another several-thousand-year-old scroll is found buried somewhere. Despite their dramatically waning membership in educated parts of your world, existing religions will fight any change in their dogma at all costs.

Stop acting like you know all of physics and all about the origin of the universe, how life sprang from non-life, the origin of consciousness, whether I exist, whether I am an unembodied mind or nature itself, etc.

Go ahead and think about these things and discuss them with your friends—it is kind of fun. But stop reaching conclusions on topics you have no way of understanding. Just realize how naive you are about almost everything. Maybe in a million years or so, you can begin addressing the big questions with some evidence. Until then, just admit what you don't know—which includes everything about Me! And please, please:

STOP MAKING STUFF UP!

As the smartest and most powerful being you know, I am not arguing for you to abandon your theistic inclinations entirely (although you can if you want). I am most interested in your using evidence to support your beliefs and being truthful about what you know and do not know. When new evidence appears and is replicated, reviewed, and accepted by experts, you should update your beliefs as warranted.

What really makes Me mad is teaching your young, impressionable children that there is an invisible, immaterial Supernatural Being(s) in the sky who created the Earth and humans, is watching what they do, and will reward them in heaven or punish them in hell based on what they believe about Holy Trinities, no God but God, angels, devils, souls, prophets in caves and New York State, burning bushes, incarnations and reincarnations, crucifixions and atonements, and that this Supernatural Being(s) needs to be worshiped and prayed to (sometimes five times a day). To this God, there is a whiff of Jonestown associated with early childhood religious education. Call Me old-fashioned, but brainwashing just feels like a bad thing to Me. Instead, I recommend some late-night stargazing, hikes in the mountains, walks on the beach, visits to art and natural history museums, etc. To the extent you can, let your kids see and experience the world.

If you had the courage of your religious convictions, you would share your values, but not your specific beliefs, until your child could understand and reflect upon what you are saying. When they approach adulthood, have a great discussion with them on what you believe and why. Listen to their response.

If your church community provides you comfort, that is great. Get together often. But do not base your social gatherings on a belief in something you have no credible evidence for and is highly unlikely to be the way you describe. Rather, base your gatherings on community, comfort, security, charity, love for each other, and family values.

Organized religions will be with you a while longer, but not that long in My grand scheme of things. I give them another thousand years at best. Forget philosophers and religious apologists. There is a reason most of them can only get jobs in universities and/or writing books, and why they use double-talk, purposely using words and phrases like epistemology, ontological, dialectic, syllogism, fideism, ethical relativism, properly basic, and supralapsarianism. You cannot reason Me into existence by sitting at your desk and coming up with falsely premised philosophical probability formulas.

Learn to be comfortable saying "I don't know. There is just not enough knowledge or evidence to make an educated statement about that, but we are working on this and other problems and making progress every day. We will keep working on them until we solve as many problems as we can."

Allow Me to conclude with an oft-quoted thought from Max Planck, the father of Quantum Theory and winner of a Nobel Prize in Physics. Planck's idea was that energy did not flow continually but was delivered in discrete packets. This revolutionary theory matched and explained actual laboratory findings. Despite this, it took almost twenty years for Planck's findings to be fully recognized and for him to be awarded the Nobel Prize. Max stated the following in his *Scientific Autobiography*:

"This experience gave me also an opportunity to learn a fact—a remarkable one, in my opinion: A new scientific truth does not triumph by convincing its opponents and making them see the light, but rather because its opponents eventually die, and a new generation grows up that is familiar with it."[106]

This view, that scientific and other truths advance due to new generations being more accepting of an idea rather than the current generation being convinced, has come to be known as Planck's principle, popularly paraphrased as, "Scientific and other truths progress one funeral at a time."

As I stated, I give you guys another fifty generations—or a little more than one thousand years—before the vast majority of you no longer belong to any organized religion. Indeed, religiously unaffiliated people in the U.S. have already risen to 30% of the population from about 5% in the 1970s. Since I am knowledgeable concerning all future human activity, I can tell you with utmost confidence that Christianity will be the first organized religion to go, while those free-thinking Muslims and Hindus will be bringing up the rear.

In the meantime, please follow the lead of your own renowned theoretical physicist and cosmologist Stephen Hawking:

"So, remember to look up at the stars and not at your feet. Try to make sense of what you see and wonder about what makes the universe exist. Be curious. And however difficult life may seem, there is always something you can do and succeed at. It matters that you don't just give up. Unleash your imagination. Shape the future."[107]

Get updates on Bob Maguire's latest projects
and follow on social media by scanning the
QR code or going to the URL below:

linktr.ee/authorbobmaguire

Appendix

Nicene Creed—the statement of belief of most mainstream Christians. Written by Orthodox Christians of the fourth century (First Council of Nicaea, 325 CE and First Council of Constantinople, 381 CE).

"I believe in one God,
the Father almighty,
maker of heaven and earth,
of all things visible and invisible.

I believe in one Lord Jesus Christ,
the Only Begotten Son of God,
born of the Father before all ages.

God from God, Light from Light,
true God from true God,
begotten, not made, consubstantial with the Father;
through him all things were made.

For us men and for our salvation
he came down from heaven,

and by the Holy Spirit was incarnate of the Virgin Mary,
and became man.

For our sake he was crucified under Pontius Pilate,
he suffered death and was buried,
and rose again on the third day
in accordance with the Scriptures.

He ascended into heaven
and is seated at the right hand of the Father.
He will come again in glory
to judge the living and the dead
and his kingdom will have no end.

I believe in the Holy Spirit, the Lord, the Giver of Life,
who proceeds from the Father and the Son,
who with the Father and the Son is adored and glorified,
who has spoken through the prophets.

I believe in one, holy, Catholic and apostolic Church.
I confess one Baptism for the forgiveness of sins
and I look forward to the resurrection of the dead
and the life of the world to come. Amen."

Things You Will Generally Not Hear in a Christian Church

1. When Christ died on the cross, the tombs of many saints opened and a couple days later the saints were resurrected and appeared to many people in the holy city (Jerusalem, I assume). So, not just Jesus was resurrected that weekend! Did these saints rise up to heaven—were they also divine? How is this event not recorded anywhere except in one of the Gospels? Could it be made-up? Are all the resurrections made-up? Were resurrections commonplace at the time?

According to Matthew 27: 51-57, "And behold, the curtain of the temple was torn in two, from top to bottom. And the earth shook, and the rocks were split. The tombs were also opened. And many bodies of the saints who had fallen asleep were raised, and coming out of the tombs after his resurrection they went into the holy city and appeared to many. When the centurion and those who were with him, keeping watch over Jesus, saw the earthquake and what took place, they were filled with awe and said, "Truly this was the Son of God!"

2. Matthew, Mark, Luke, and John were not written by the disciples and followers of Christ named Matthew, Mark, Luke, and John. They were written in Greek some thirty-five to sixty-five years after the death of Christ. All four were written anonymously with the modern names of the four evangelists added in the second century. Only eight of the twenty-seven books of the New Testament are almost certain to have been written by the people traditionally thought to be their authors.[108]

There are "no contemporary sources for the life of Jesus and his ministry, no one at the time wrote anything down. Contrary to popular belief, the Gospels were not written by the disciples of Jesus. In fact, the Gospels existed for about a hundred years prior to later Christians assigning names and authorship to them."[109]

3. Denova notes that the human versus divine nature of Christ was not resolved until the Council of Chalcedon in 451 CE. After much discussion, the issue was decided, and Jesus was declared to be of two natures, simultaneously human and divine. The two natures remained separate and distinct elements of Jesus of Nazareth. Yes, this was decided by church leaders in 451 CE.

4. It is well known that before the Gospels of the New Testament were written, the first followers of Jesus wrote another kind of book containing the sayings of Jesus. This "sayings gospel" has been referred to as "Q," and this source was used by both Matthew and Luke. The Q scholar Burton L. Mack concludes that a thorough reading of Q creates conflicts between stories told in the Gospels of Matthew, Mark, Luke, and John, and the history they record. Therefore, the narrative Gospels no longer should be read as the actual records of historical events that generated Christianity. From Q it is clear that the earliest followers of Jesus had no knowledge of many of the events upon which the narrative Gospels are based, such as the baptism of Jesus, the ill will between him and the Jewish authorities and their plot to kill him, Jesus' various instructions to the disciples, his transfiguration, march to Jerusalem, last supper, trial, and crucifixion as king of the Jews, and finally, and perhaps critically, the finding of an empty tomb and Jesus' resurrection from the dead. Mack concludes that these events should be accounted for as mythmaking.[110]

5. The Bible is not inerrant. It contains many historically inaccurate and contradictory statements. Many of these inaccuracies are important.[111]

6. The majority of scholars in Europe and North America have understood Jesus as a Jewish apocalyptic prophet

who preached preparation for the coming of the Son of Man and the Kingdom of God which was to come during his disciples' lifetimes.[112] Oops!

7. Jesus was not an only child. He had brothers and sisters who are mentioned in the Bible by Mark and Matthew:

"Is not this the carpenter, the son of Mary and brother of James and Joses and Judas and Simon, and are not his sisters here with us?" (Mark 6:3)

"Is not this the carpenter's son? Is not his mother called Mary? And are not his brothers James and Joseph and Simon and Judas? And are not all his sisters with us?" (Matthew 13:55-56)

8. Some Christians including members of the Catholic Church, some Lutherans, Anglicans, and other Protestants, adhere to the doctrine of the perpetual virginity, wherein the siblings mentioned in the Bible were cousins of Jesus or prior children of Joseph. Indeed, the Second Council of Constantinople in 553 gave Mary the title Aeiparthenos, which means "perpetual virgin." Well, they should know!

9. Americans are losing their religion.[113] In a survey conducted in 2023 by the non-partisan Public Religion Research Institute, 26% of Americans consider them-

selves to be unaffiliated with a religion. That number has increased by 5% in just ten years while white Evangelical Protestants have increased 0.1%, white mainline non-Evangelical Protestants have decreased 4.4%, white Catholics have decreased by 6%, and Hispanic Catholics have decreased by 3.4%.

Only 64% of Americans now identify as Christians.

Only 53% of respondents say religion is important in their lives versus 72% in 2013.

Gallup also reports that in 2023 an average of 30% of U.S. adults attended religious services weekly vs. 42% twenty years previously.[114]

Works Cited

1. Benjamin Wormald, "The Future of World Religions: Population Growth Projections, 2010-2050," Pew Research Center's Religion & Public Life Project, April 2, 2015.

2. Barbara Ryden and Bradley M. Peterson, *Foundation of Astrophysics* (San Francisco, CA: Pearson Education, Inc., Pearson Addison-Wesley Publishers, 2011), 194.

3. Ibid., 203.

4. Ibid., 436.

5. Ibid., 398.

6. Daniel Simberloff, "Roundtable: A Modern Mass Extinction?", WGBH Educational Foundation and Clear Blue Sky Productions, Inc., 2001, https://www.pbs.org/wgbh/evolution/extinction/massext/statement_03.html.

7. "Six Million Years of Human Evolution," in *Human Evolution*, Smithsonian National Museum of Natural History, naturalhistory.si.edu.

8. G. Miller and Scott Spoolman, *Environmental Science—Biodiversity Is a Crucial Part of the Earth's Natural Capital* (Cengage Learning, 2012), 62.

9. Yinon M. Bar-on, Rob Phillips, and Ron Milo, "The Biomass Distribution on Earth," *PNAS* 115, no. 25, May 21, 2018, 6506-6511.

10. Natalie Angier, "What's Creepy, Crawly and Big in Movies?", *The New York Times*, Section 1, February 18, 1993, 13.

11. "Numbers of Insects (Species and Individuals)," Smithsonian Institution, Information Sheet Number 18, 1996, si.edu.

12. Michael Jordan, *Encyclopedia of Gods: Over 2,500 Deities of the World*, 1993.

13. Gary Wenk, Ph.D., "Psychology Today: Why Do Humans Keep Inventing Gods to Worship?", reviewed by Ekua Hagan, July 6, 2021.

14. Wikipedia contributors, "List of Roman deities," *Wikipedia, The Free Encyclopedia*, accessed August 15, 2024, https://en.wikipedia.org/w/index.php?title=List_of_Roman_deities&oldid=1235474755.

15. *Catechism of the Catholic Church*, 2nd ed. (Libreria Editrice Vaticana, 2019), 105, DV11, 31.

16. Ibid., 745-747, 196.

17. *Baltimore Catechism One* (The Order of The Third Plenary Council of Baltimore, 1885; rev. ed. 1993, repr., TAN Books, 2010), 9.

18. *Catechism of the Catholic Church*, 2nd ed. (Libreria Editrice Vaticana, 2019), 2225, 537.

19. Richard L. Bushman, "Joseph Smith: American Religious Leader (1805-1844)," *Encyclopedia Britannica*, accessed January 23, 2024.

20. Robert L. Millet, "What Latter-day Saints Believe About Jesus Christ," address to Harvard Divinity School, March 2021.

21. Elizabeth Chuck, "What are the Differences Between Sunni and Shiite Muslims," NBC News, January 4, 2016.

22. Mark W. Muesse, "Great World Religions: Hinduism," Lecture 2, The Teaching Company, 2003.

23. Neha Sahgal et al., "Religion In India: Tolerance And Segregation," Pew Research Center survey, June 29, 2021.

24. Mark W. Muesse, "Great World Religions: Hinduism," Lecture 3, The Teaching Company, 2003.

25. Neha Sahgal et al., "Religion In India: Tolerance And Segregation."

26. Mark W. Muesse, "Great World Religions: Hinduism," Lecture 9, The Teaching Company, 2003.

27. Malcolm David Eckel, *Great World Religions: Buddhism*, Course Guidebook, The Teaching Company, 2003.

28. The World Counts, Copenhagen, Denmark and Cancer Statistics, National Cancer Institute, September 25, 2020.

29. St. Augustine, *Enchiridion* 3, 11: PL40, 236.

30. William Lane Craig, "Is the Foundation of Morality Natural or Supernatural? The Craig-Harris Debate," University of Notre Dame, April 2011.

31. William Lane Craig, "The Indispensability of Theological Meta-Ethical Foundations for Morality," *Reasonable Faith*.

32. Samuel Harris, *The Moral Landscape: How Science Can Determine Human Values* (New York, NY: Free Press, 2010).

33. T. Ylä-Anttila, "Comparative Moral Principles: Justifications, Values, and Foundations," *Humanit Soc Sci Commun* 10, no. 199, 2023.

34. Jonathan Haidt and Jesse Graham, "When Morality Opposes Justice: Conservatives Have Moral Intuitions That Liberals May Not Recognize," *Soc Just Res* 20, no. 1, 2007, 98–116, https://doi.org/10.1007/s11211-007-0034-z.

35. William Lane Craig, "The Problem of Evil and Suffering," Lectures at Gracepoint Church, *Reasonable Faith*.

36. Craig, "The Problem of Evil and Suffering," *Reasonable Faith*.

37. Richard Swinburne, "The Coherence of Theism," in *Philosophers on God: Talking About Existence* (London, UK: Bloomsbury Academic, 2024).

38. Alvin Plantinga, "Supralapsarianism, or 'O Felix Culpa'" posted by Andrew M. Bailey, https://andrewmbailey.com.

39. Daniel C. Dennett and Alvin Plantinga, *Science and Religion: Are They Compatible?* (Oxford University Press, 2011).

40. Lydia B. Amir, *Humor and the Good Life in Modern Philosophy: Shaftesbury, Hamann, Kierkegaard* (SUNY Press), 81.

41. *Catechism of the Catholic Church*, 2nd ed. (Libreria Editrice Vaticana, 2019), 396-397, 100.

42. Ibid., 416, 105.

43. Ibid., 417, 105.

44. Anselm, *Cur Deus Homo: Why God Became Man*, trans. by Sidney Norton Deane (Pantianos Classics, 1903).

45. William Lane Craig, "Doctrine of Man (Part 12)," *Defenders* Podcast Series 2, Reasonable Faith, December 1, 2013.

46. Bart D. Ehrman, *Jesus, Interrupted: Revealing the Hidden Contradictions in the Bible (and Why We Don't Know About Them)* (HarperCollins, 2009).

47. Anselm, *Cur Deus Homo: Why God Became Man*, trans. by Sidney Norton Deane (Pantianos Classics, 1903).

48. J. Hashmi, "Grace, Faith and Works (Part 1 of 4): The Components of Faith," February 4, 2008, last modified October 4, 2009, https://www.islamreligion.com/.

49. William Lane Craig, "Question of the Week Q&A #479: What Does it Mean to Say God Is a Soul?", Reasonable Faith, June 19, 2016.

50. *Catechism of the Catholic Church*, 2nd ed. (Libreria Editrice Vaticana, 2019), 1261, 321.

51. G.E. Jarvis, "Estimating Limits for Natural Human Embryo Mortality," *F1000Res*, August 26, 2016.

52. Syama Allard, "5 Things to Know About Hindus and Death" (Hindu American Foundation, September 3, 2020).

53. "Richard Dawkins and Catholic Cardinal George Pell Discuss Religion, Morals and Evolution on Q&A," Scraps from the Loft, March 1, 2019.

54. Justin Taylor, "An FAQ from J. P. Moreland on the Human Soul," *TGC U.S. Edition Blogs*, August 31, 2016.

55. *Catechism of the Catholic Church*, 2nd ed. (Libreria Editrice Vaticana, 2019), 93.

56. Ed Jarrett, October 11, 2023, https://www.christianity.com/.

57. *Catechism of the Catholic Church*, 2nd ed. (Libreria Editrice Vaticana, 2019), 1996.

58. Ibid., 1997.

59. Ibid., 2005.

60. Rebecca Denova, "Sources for the Life & Ministry of Jesus: Christianity as a Legal Religion, and the Divine Nature of Jesus," *World History Encyclopedia*, January 5, 2021.

61. *Catechism of the Catholic Church*, 2nd ed. (Libreria Editrice Vaticana, 2019), 334-336, 87.

62. William Lane Craig, "The Origin of Satan," as recorded in "Doctrine of Creation," Part 22, Reasonable Faith, 2018.

63. Islamic Networks Group, "Question #74: What Does Islam Say about Satan," in "Answers to Frequently Asked Questions About Islam and Muslims," San Jose, CA, ing.org.

64. *Catechism of the Catholic Church*, 2nd ed. (Libreria Editrice Vaticana, 2019), 685, Glossary, 882.

65. NPR/TED Staff and Sean Carroll, "Why Does Time Exist?", *Ted Radio Hour*, June 19, 2015.

66. Jason Dulle, "Is an Unembodied Mind too Abstract a Notion to be the Cause of the Universe?", https://www.onenesspentecostal.com/unembodiedmind.htm.

67. David J. Chalmers, *Reality+: Virtual Worlds and the Problems of Philosophy* (W. W. Norton & Company, Inc., 2022), 260-263.

68. Sayyid Moustafa Al-Qazwini, *Discovering Islam* (Islamic Educational Center of Orange County, 2001).

69. Mohammad Aly Sergie, "The Sunni-Shia Divide," *Council on Foreign Relations*, April 27, 2023.

70. C.S. Lewis, *Mere Christianity* (Harper Collins, 1952).

71. William Lane Craig, "The Problem of Evil and Suffering," "What About Those Who have Never Heard," Reasonable Faith, March 9, 2008.

72. C. Mora, D. P. Tittensor, S. Adl, A. G. Simpson, & B. Worm, "How Many Species Are There on Earth and in the Ocean?" *PLoS Biol* 9(8): e1001127, 2011.

73. History.com Editors, "Religions on the End of the World," A&E Television Networks, November 6, 2009, https//.history.com/topics/religion/religions-on-the-end-of-the-world.

74. Daniel J. Hill, "Why God Matters," *Philosophers On God: Talking about Existence*, 6-7.

75. *Baltimore Catechism One* (The Order of The Third Plenary Council of Baltimore, 1885; rev. ed. 1993, repr., TAN Books, 2010), 7.

76. Anselm, *Cur Deus Homo: Why God Became Man*, translated by Sidney Norton Deane (Pantianos Classics, 1903).

77. Richard Dawkins, "Why I am an Atheist," *Philosophers On God: Talking about Existence*, 88.

78. Daniel Dennett, "Breaking the Spell," *Philosophers On God: Talking about Existence*, 122.

79. Daniel J. Hill, "Why God Matters," *Philosophers on God: Talking About Existence*, 3.

80. Richard Swinburne, "The Coherence of Theism," *Philosophers on God: Talking About Existence*, 14.

81. David J. Chalmers, *Reality+: Virtual Worlds and the Problems of Philosophy* (New York, NY: W. W. Norton & Company, Inc., 2022), 130-131.

82. St. Thomas Aquinas, Opusc. xiv, Exposition, *de Divinis Nominibus*, iv, lect. 2.

83. St. Thomas Aquinas, *I Contra Gentes*, 42.

84. E. Larson and L. Witham, "Leading Scientists Still Reject God," *Nature* 394, 1998, 313.

85. Ian A. Hatton, Eric D. Galbraith, Nono S. C. Merleau, and Jeffery A. Shander, "The Human Cell Count and Size Distribution," PNAS DOI:10.1073/ pnas.23030 77120, Stanford University, 2023, https://www.pnas. org/doi/10.1073/pnas.2303077120.

86. Francis S. Collins, *The Language of God: A Scientist Presents Evidence for Belief* (New York, NY: Free Press, a division of Simon and Schuster, Inc., 2006).

87. C.S. Lewis, *Mere Christianity*.

88. C.S. Lewis, *Mere Christianity*.

89. Collins, *The Language of God: A Scientist Presents Evidence for Belief*.

90. Ibid.

91. Ibid.

92. Ibid.

93. William Lane Craig, "Is the Foundation of Morality Natural or Supernatural? The Craig-Harris Debate," University of Notre Dame, April 2011.

94. William Lane Craig and James White, "Molinism vs. Calvinism: The Problem of Evil," debate at University of Notre Dame, April 2011.

95. Craig and White, "Molinism vs. Calvinism: The Problem of Evil," April 2011.

96. Julius Caesar, accessed December 18, 2023, <u>Quotationspage.com</u>.

97. Demosthenes, accessed 2023, <u>https://www.brainyquote.com/quotes/demosthenes_154835</u>.

98. Jonathan Haidt, *The Righteous Mind: Why Good People Are Divided by Politics and Religion* (London, UK: Penguin Books, 2012), xiv-xv.

99. Ibid., xv.

100. Ibid., 34.

101. The World Economic Forum—Humanitarian Action, Visual Capitalist, April 4, 2022.

102. U.S. Government Accountability Office, "Fusion Energy: Potentially Transformative Technology Still Faces Fundamental Challenges," GAO-23-105813, March 30, 2023.

103. Yinon M. Bar-On, Rob Phillips, and Ron Milo, "The Biomass Distribution on Earth," *Proceedings of the National Academy of Sciences* 115, no. 25, May 21, 2018, 6506-6511.

104. Fran Dorey, "*Homo sapiens*—Modern Humans," Australian Museum, October 16, 2020.

105. History.com editors, "Neolithic Revolution," January 12, 2018, updated October 4, 2023, https://www.history.com/topics/prehistoric-age/neolithic-revolution.

106. Max Planck, *The Origin and Development of the Quantum Theory: with "A Scientific Autobiography,"* trans. Ludvik Silberstein and Hans Thacher Clarke (Amazon Kindle Direct Publishing, December 3, 2012).

107. Stephen Hawking, *Brief Answers to the Big Questions* (Hachette, October 13, 2018).

108. Bart D. Ehrman, *Jesus, Interrupted: Revealing the Hidden Contradictions in the Bible (and Why We Don't Know About Them)* (New York, NY: HarperCollins Publishers, 2009).

109. Rebecca Denova, "Sources for the Life & Ministry of Jesus: Christianity as a Legal Religion, and the Divine Nature of Jesus," *World History Encyclopedia*, January 5, 2021.

110. Burton L. Mack, *The Lost Gospel of Q and Christian Origins* (San Francisco: Harper San Francisco, 1993).

111. Ehrman, *Jesus, Interrupted* (New York, NY: Harper-Collins, 2010).

112. Ibid.

113. Russel Contreras, "Americans Continue to Lose Their Religion as GOP Pushes It," *Axios*, Politics and Policy, March 29, 2024.

114. Jeffrey M. Jones, "Church Attendance Has Declined in Most U.S. Religious Groups," *Gallup News*, March 25, 2024.

Excerpts from Jonathan Haidt, *The Righteous Mind: Why Good People Are Divided by Politics and Religion* (London, UK: Penguin Books, 2012), Copyright © Jonathan Haidt, 2012, are printed with permission.

Excerpts from William Lane Craig, Reasonable Faith are printed with permission.

Acknowledgements

I would like to thank a number of people who helped me in the writing and editing of this book. Several trusted acquaintances performed in-depth reviews of a near-final version of the work, including my brother Hugh Maguire, brother-in-law Joseph Toto, and good friends Maddy Franchi and Deb Mitchell. Their many insightful comments led to significant improvements in the final product. Many thanks to Kristine Ochu for introducing me to Brian Skillen of Publishing Hackers and his co-workers, the awesome Whale Kangas, my editor and all-around book publishing guide, Michael Brewer-Berres, formatter and social media guru, and Tatiana Vila of Vila Design (eBook and Book Cover Design). Without their contributions, this book would surely not have come to fruition.